Dessert Champ Creamy Obsessions

Copyright ©2023, Recipes for Daily Bread Publishing

©Diane Roark

All Rights Reserved

Editor: Donna Toler

Contributing Editor: Terry Toler, terry@terrytoler.com

Cover design: jibankhan, Graphic Designer

Food Stylist: Karen Johnson

Food Photographer: Bonnie Rose Photography and World Food Championships.

For information or bookings email: dianeroark8484@gmail.com

First U.S. Edition: April 2023

Printed in the United States of America

Paperback ISBN: 979-8-9867209-3-7

Hardback ISBN: 979-8-9867209-4-4

꙰

Thank you for purchasing this Dessert Champ Creamy Obsessions cookbook from best-selling author, Diane Roark. As an additional thank you, Diane would like to send you free gifts periodically.

If you'd like to receive:

Newsletters

Updates

New Releases

Announcements

Recipes

Sign up at: https://wandering-butterfly-4036.ck.page/1d860b2617/

Follow Diane at:

Facebook: https://www.facebook.com/recipesforourdailybread/

Instagram: https://www.instagram.com/recipesforourbread/

Other Books By Diane Roark

Heartaches to Blessings

Big Dreams Journal

Forgiveness Journal

https://www.amazon.com/dp/B0BBBVR2RX

AWARDS/RECOGNITION

2017 Finished 3rd in dessert at the World Food Championships with a rare perfect score.

2017 Finished 2nd in a dessert competition on the TODAY Show.

2017 Top 10 at National Banana Pudding Festival.

2018 Top 10 at National Banana Pudding Festival.

2018 Finished 5th in dessert at the World Food Championships with a rare perfect score.

2019 Finished 4th in dessert at the World Food Championships.

2020 World Food Championships was canceled due to Covid.

2021 Finished 5th in dessert at World Food Championships.

2022 Finished 7th in dessert at World Food Championships.

DEDICATION

I dedicate this cookbook to God first, who planted in me the ideas and recipes. He gives me the ability to know what to do, the strength to do it, and the endurance to complete it.

Thank you, Lord, for being my Savior and being with me daily to accomplish the Big Dreams you have given me.

To my readers who don't have time to bake, you can whip up these easy recipes quickly.

Food brings people together. There's nothing better than seeing a smile on someone's face after eating a homemade dessert. Without saying a word it says "I love you" and "You're special."

When you share your baked goods, you'll be making a memory to last a lifetime and getting a chance to encourage someone. You can do it!

To my readers who dream big, keep dreaming! God has placed dreams in your heart. Let him guide you to accomplishing them. You can do anything you set your heart to do with God's help.

Ask him daily for his help, and you'll be successful. After all, He gave you the dream. Why would He give it to you if you couldn't accomplish it?

If you need some encouragement, read my memoir, Heartaches to Blessings. I talk a lot about the heartaches in my life and how God overwhelmed me with his love and got me through them.

One of those dreams was beyond what I could've ever asked for. He allowed me to compete in the World Food Championships. I've made it into the top ten each year, which gave me a golden ticket to compete the following year.

If God can make my dreams come true, He can make yours come true as well.

Do Your Best and Let God Do The Rest!

DREAM BIG!

With Love, Diane

How sweet are your words to my taste, sweeter than honey to my mouth! Psalm 119:103 (NIV)

TABLE OF CONTENTS

INTRODUCTION

I'm a mother of five adult children, including a special needs son who has had seventeen brain surgeries. We have twins and two adopted children. Baking has always been my passion, but when my kids were young, I had little time to bake. I understand the need for easy no-bake desserts.

A lot of the easy recipes in this book were popular on my Quick & Easy recipe blog. I had it for ten years. My followers were at all levels of baking expertise. Some wanted more difficult and sophisticated recipes. A majority expressed a desire for easy no-bake desserts and made-from-scratch desserts with the same flavors.

This cookbook has a little of both. It also includes competition secrets for making light and creamy pies, custards, puddings, trifles, sauces, and more.

Most of all, they taste good! You'll love the lush creamy textures with the contrast of crunchy additions of pralines, cookies, and toasted nuts. Every layer of your dessert should taste awesome. Don't say it includes a flavor if you can't taste it. The layers in these recipes are flavorful. Your mouth will instantly tell your brain you can taste the flavor indicated in the title. For this reason, you will find spices to elevate even the simple graham cracker crust.

I've included recipes that I've used at the World Food Championships. The ones that helped me finish in the top ten in the dessert category five years in a row. I'm going to show you how to make them and have your family eating out of your hand. Pun intended.

For those who have never heard of the World Food Championships, it is a five-day cooking competition where the best chefs and home cooks from all over the world compete in three rounds of cooking. Each Category Champion wins $7,500. Category champions compete again at the final table, where they can win the World Food Champion title and an additional $100,000.

I've never won the whole thing. Someday!

Dessert is not the only category. Others include Bacon, Barbecue, Burger, Rice/Noodle, Sandwich, Seafood, Soup, Steak, and Vegetarian. There are forty-five chefs in each category. They qualified by winning a sanctioned event, so the competition is stiff. So these recipes have to be good.

This Creamy Dessert Cookbook includes easy no-bake recipes plus made-from-scratch recipes with the same flavors. Both versions of recipes are light, creamy, and delicious.

I've refined them over the years and compiled the creamy desserts into this cookbook. I've made a lot of mistakes over the years. Hopefully, you can learn from my mistakes and make dreamy desserts on your first attempt.

The pies are massive but will pile high in a deep dish pie crust. The cheesecakes are tall, with brownies or blondies stacked high on top. The peanut butter pie has peanut butter balls mounded high on it. Being a food judge with the E.A.T (Execute, Appearance, Taste) methodology at the World Food Championships, I know the importance of appearance. You eat first with your eyes. Beautiful desserts grab your attention and make you want to take a bite.

That's exactly what I want to help you do by helping your dish make a grand appearance. So everyone will want to take a bite.

I love taking an easy dessert and making it even better with an added ingredient. To do this, I use homemade sauces including:

1. Caramel Sauce
2. Butterscotch Sauce
3. Praline Sauce
4. Chocolate Sauce
5. Vanilla Sauce (Creme Anglaise)
6. White Chocolate Sauce
7. Berry Sauces

For texture, I add:

1. Homemade Brownie or Blondie pieces
2. Peanut Butter Balls
3. Candy
4. Chocolate Decorations
5. Toasted Nuts
6. Nut Brittles
7. Cookies
8. Crunchy Cereal
9. Pretzels

To top off desserts, I often add flavored whipped cream piped or stacked high on a pie, cheesecake, or dessert plate.

All of these things turn a simple dessert into something special.

It's so much fun!

SHORTCUTS & TIPS FOR NO-BAKE DESSERTS

Let's start with something simple.

You don't always have time to make your desserts from scratch. I've made lots of no-bake desserts when time didn't allow it. They not only save time but can be delicious and comforting.

No-bake desserts can include frozen whipped topping, cream cheese, instant pudding mixes, and cookie pie crusts.

Be sure to purchase instant pudding and not Cook n Serve pudding mix.

Thaw cream cheese and frozen whipped topping before using them. Don't thaw the frozen whipped topping in the microwave. I've made that mistake before. You'll most likely get a runny mess.

It's important to use softened cream cheese. It's easier to work with, and you'll get a much creamier dessert.

How do you have a no-bake dessert with a pie crust? I've included easy cookie-crust and graham-cracker recipes. You don't have to bake them. Instead, refrigerate the crust for three to four hours until firm.

Graham Cracker or Cookie Crust Pie Tip

Use a small food processor and grind the cookies or crackers into fine crumbs. You can also crush them by placing them in a ziplock bag. Put the bag on a towel and use something hard like a rolling pin or frying pan to crush the cookies. When using stuffed cookies for a crust, they require less butter since they have a filling.

HOMEMADE PIE CRUST RECIPE AND TIPS

My dad was a firm believer that apple cider vinegar was good for everything. I didn't believe him back then but found it true when making pie crust. There's a noticeable difference in the flakiness. Vinegar helps tenderize pie dough. It only takes a small amount of it in the dough, so you won't taste it and no one will know that the "secret ingredient" is apple cider vinegar.

The following things work together to achieve a beautiful pie crust:

- Keep your butter cold. Remove it from the refrigerator just before grating it.
- Yes, grate your butter on a cheese grater.
- Don't touch the butter when grating it. It will get too soft.
- Add ice water, a little at a time.
- Use your hands as little as possible. The heat from your hands will melt the cold butter before it's put in the oven. I often wear gloves. If using parchment paper, use the extra to fold the dough over.
- Bring the dough together into a disk. It will be a little crumbly but still forms a disk easily.
- The dough can be easily overworked. As long as it's mostly holding together, you don't need to spend a lot of time kneading it.
- Chill in disks with round, smooth edges. You can do this after wrapping it in plastic before placing it in the refrigerator. Pressing the sides will smooth them out.

FLAKY DOUBLE-CRUST PIE CRUST RECIPE

INGREDIENTS

- 3 cups all-purpose flour, 390 grams
- 2 tablespoons sugar
- 1 teaspoon salt
- 3/4 cup Crisco shortening
- 1/2 cup butter
- 1 tablespoon vinegar
- 8 tablespoons ice water, prepare a cup of ice water

INSTRUCTIONS

1. Whisk the sugar and salt into the flour.
2. Cut the small pinches of shortening into the flour using a pastry cutter or a fork.
3. Use a grater and grate the cold butter into the flour and shortening.
4. Make a well in the center of the flour mixture.
5. Add the vinegar and ice water to the center of the flour mixture.
6. Slowly pull the dry ingredients a little at a time from the sides into the center until you incorporate all the ingredients.
7. Form the dough into a ball, touching the dough as little as possible.
8. This recipe makes two pie crusts.
9. Cut the dough into two equal pieces and shape it into two disks.
10. Cover with plastic wrap.
11. Refrigerate for twenty to thirty minutes.
12. Roll out on a lightly floured surface. Flour the rolling pin too.
13. Roll the dough out lightly from the center. After a couple of rolls, pick your dough up and turn it at forty-five degrees. Keep rolling until the dough is 1-1/2 to 2 inches larger than your pie plate. Be sure to release pressure and lift the rolling pin before you get to the end of the dough. It will help keep the edges from splitting or cracking.
14. If rolling your dough out on parchment paper or a small silicon mat, pick the entire thing up and flip it over on the pie plate. You can also roll the dough up on your rolling pin and place it over an ungreased pie dish. Don't pull or stretch your dough. Use a bent index finger to fit dough into the bottom edges of the pie dish.
15. When crimping the edges, tuck them under.
16. Unbaked pie shells can be wrapped in plastic wrap with aluminum foil over the plastic.
17. Can be frozen for up to two months.

PARTIALLY BAKED PIE CRUST

A "blind-baked crust" is cooked until lightly tan to keep the filling from turning the bottom of the crust soggy. Cooking the blind-bake too far will cause the crust to burn when baking the filling. Preheat the oven to 400 F. degrees.

Place the pie shell on a baking sheet. Line the pie with parchment paper and fill it with dried beans, rice, or pie weights.

Bake the pie crust for twelve minutes. If the filling needs to be cooked, bake it for six to seven minutes. The dough should look dry but not browned. Remove from the oven. Remove the beans, rice, or pie weights and the parchment paper. Let the crust cool completely. After the beans or rice cools, save them to use next time.

PURE VANILLA EXTRACT

Use pure vanilla extract or vanilla paste which gives the dish even more flavor. A tablespoon of vanilla paste equals one vanilla whole bean. When making a vanilla pudding, custard, or pastry cream use pure vanilla paste if not using a whole bean. The flavor is more intense and perfect for vanilla desserts. The vanilla paste can be heated with the milk. If using vanilla extract, add it after removing the custard from the stove.

CRUNCHY LAYER TIPS

Every dessert needs a crunchy layer, including creamy desserts. Desserts are always sweet, so balancing textures in a dessert is so important. When you hit the sweet spot of a crunchy layer with a light and creamy layer you are on your way to a perfect score.

All desserts need a little salt, it brings out the flavors in your dessert. The crunchy layer is a great place to add salt.

CREAMY DESSERT LAYER TIPS & RECIPE

What's the difference between custard, American pudding, and pastry cream?

The main difference is what you do with it. Custards may be served warm, but pastry cream is served cold. These creamy desserts use basic ingredients, but the technique can be challenging, it can easily be too stiff or runny. Custards are thickened with egg yolks, while pudding and pastry cream are both thickened with egg yolks and cornstarch or flour. It is difficult to achieve a consistent result without cornstarch or flour.

You can use pastry cream and custard to fill doughnuts, cakes, pies, tarts, cream puffs, eclairs, Napoleons, Boston Cream pie, and other pastries. It is the base for Crème Brulee or ice cream.

Flavor these desserts with wet and dry stir-ins like chocolate, coffee, hazelnut, liqueurs, and zests. You can infuse flavor into the cream by soaking the cream in popcorn, candy, cookies, tea bags, herbs, etc.

Heat your cream or milk with the add-ins until you see bubbles start to foam on the top. Turn off the heat and let the cream sit until it's cooled to room temperature. The longer the mixture sits, the more flavorful it becomes.

Milk will burn if not constantly watched on the stove. The best way to heat the milk or cream is in the microwave. Strain out the solids and continue using the infused cream in your recipe.

Pudding is made with milk or half-and-half, and thickened with flour or cornstarch like a pastry cream, but it's much sweeter. My desserts are sweetened with more sugar than in a French bakery. For this reason, they are considered homemade puddings.

If you like your desserts less sweet, try making the pastry cream using 1/3 cup of sugar to 2 cups of half-and-half or milk. I've even seen them made with ¼ cup of sugar to 2 cups of milk.

SUGAR SUBSTITUTE

At the World Food Championships in 2021, I was required to use Pyure stevia instead of sugar. With the stevia, I added a little maple syrup to sweeten and flavor my apple dessert. It worked well and is a great alternative to sugar.

TEMPERING EGGS

The tricky part of making pastry cream or pudding is tempering the egg mixture. If you pour your egg mixture straight into a hot liquid, you'll end up with pieces of scrambled eggs. Tempering your eggs will help prevent it.

Here's how to do it. Place your bowl on a silicone mat or towel to steady it. Whisk the egg yolks and cornstarch until light and fluffy. Pour one to two cups of the warm milk into the egg mixture while whisking vigorously. Then add the egg mixture back into the warm milk. Then immediately pour the mixture into a clean pot on the stove while still whisking.

Have everything you need ready so you can work quickly. Place your whisk and bowl with the eggs near your saucepan. Have your vanilla and butter ready too. Keep whisking the pot, and make sure you get into the corner of the pot where the liquid can easily burn. Use a silicone spatula to scrape down the sides of the pot where it can also burn.

Here's the recipe:

PUDDING

INGREDIENTS

- 4 egg yolks
- 1/4 cup cornstarch
- 1/8 teaspoon salt
- 2 cups half-and-half
- 3/4 cup sugar
- 1 tablespoon pure vanilla paste
- 2 tablespoons butter
- ½ cup heavy cream

INSTRUCTIONS

1. Whisk egg yolks until a pale-yellow color. Whisk in cornstarch and salt. Once the egg yolks and cornstarch are light and smooth, it's ready for the milk.
2. Heat the half-and-half, sugar, and vanilla in the microwave for about three to four minutes. The milk should be steaming but not boiling. You have less chance of burning it that way. Traditionally, the milk is heated on the stove. This is faster. I use a glass measuring bowl with a handle to heat the milk. Be careful removing it from the microwave and stirring it. Air bubbles may pop when stirring.
3. Temper Eggs: Place a silicone mat or a towel under your bowl to prevent it from slipping. Slowly drizzle the steaming milk over the egg mixture while constantly whisking. You will use one hand to drizzle the milk into the egg yolks and one hand to whisk the mixture. Once the bottom of the bowl is warm, whisk in the remaining warm milk.
4. Pour the mixture into a clean pot and whisk over medium-low heat until it thickens. Use a whisk in one hand and a silicone spatula in the other. Remember to rub the spatula around the edges of the pot from time to time so the cream on the sides, corners, and bottom of the pot doesn't burn.
5. Cook while constantly whisking until the pudding is glossy and thick. Remove the pudding from the heat.
6. Add butter and whisk until the butter is completely melted and incorporated.
7. If your pudding is lumpy, no worries! Push it through a strainer or use an immersion blender to make sure it is smooth without lumps. This is a trick I do in food competitions. It's faster than using a fine strainer.
8. Put the pudding in a clean bowl to cool. Cover with plastic wrap touching the surface. To cool quickly, set the bowl inside a larger bowl filled with ice water.
9. Once at room temperature, refrigerate until thick.
10. Remove from the refrigerator and whisk it well.
11. Whip the heavy cream to stiff peaks and fold it in the pudding for a light and creamy pudding.

HOMEMADE WHIPPED CREAM TIPS, INCLUDING STABILIZED WHIPPED CREAM

Whipped Cream is a standard inside or on creamy desserts. Homemade whipped cream can take your dessert from good to fabulous. You could also use frozen whipped topping. Just make sure you let it thaw before using it.

PRO TIP - Chilling the bowl, beaters, and heavy cream is a great way to speed up the whipping process. Place them in the freezer for at least fifteen minutes.

Heavy cream can be whipped in minutes. It can easily be flavored. My favorite way to flavor whipped cream is by turning freeze-dried berries into powder which adds flavor. You simply use a food processor to grind the freeze-dried fruit into powder and then add it to the whipped cream. The fruit adds loads of flavor and color.

PRO TIP - Use freeze-dried fruit powder to flavor whipped cream, cheesecakes, buttercream, yogurt, pudding, custards, smoothies, chocolate, and more.

Decorating my desserts with whipped cream is one of my favorite things to do. Top your desserts with homemade whipped cream just before serving or pipe whipped cream to decorate your dessert. To pipe, you'll need to stabilize it first to help with structure.

Many of my recipes include piped whipped cream. To pipe whip cream, it has to hold its structure. If you stabilize your whipped cream, you can pipe it the same as you would buttercream.

You can achieve a stabilized whipped cream in several ways. Make sure you're using heavy cream with high-fat content. Whipping cream has less fat. The higher the fat content the better it will whip.

STABILIZE WHIPPED CREAM USING POWDERED SUGAR

Confectioner's sugar includes cornstarch which stabilizes the whipped cream. You need to increase your powdered sugar. It will give you a sweeter cream but is stable enough to pipe. Whipping it slowly incorporates small air bubbles into the cream, which results in a more stable and sturdy whipped cream. Larger air bubbles will deflate easier.

If you plan on piping your whipped cream, especially when making flowers, you need a 2:1 ratio.

INGREDIENTS

- 1 cup heavy cream
- 1/2 cup powdered sugar
- 1 teaspoon pure vanilla paste or extract

INSTRUCTIONS

1. Put all the ingredients in a large cold mixing bowl.
2. Mix on low speed until ingredients are combined.
3. Mix on medium speed until soft peaks form, scraping the sides of the bowl often.
4. Mix on high speed until stiff peaks form.
5. When you raise your mixer, the peaks should form and not fall back into themselves when you hold your beaters upright.
6. Don't overwhip your cream. It will turn into butter.

STABILIZED WHIPPED CREAM USING CREAM CHEESE

INGREDIENTS

- 1 cup heavy cream
- 1/3 cup powdered sugar
- 1 teaspoon pure vanilla
- 4 ounces of cream cheese

INSTRUCTIONS

1. Put the heavy cream, sugar, and vanilla in a large mixing bowl.
2. Mix on low speed until ingredients are combined.
3. Mix on medium speed until soft peaks form. Scrap the sides of the bowl often.
4. Add dollops of cream cheese.
5. Mix on high speed until stiff peaks form.

STABILIZED WHIPPED CREAM USING INSTANT PUDDING MIX

This method is a shortcut to adding flavor and stabilizing whipped cream. Any instant pudding flavor will work. It's a fabulous trick and adds lots of flavor and stability.

INGREDIENTS

- 2 cups heavy whipping cream
- 3 tablespoons Instant Pudding Mix (dry powder)
- 1 teaspoon vanilla extract
- 1/4 cup powdered sugar

INSTRUCTIONS

1. Put all the ingredients in a large mixing bowl.
2. Mix on low speed until ingredients are combined.
3. Mix on high speed until stiff peaks form. Scrap the sides of the bowl often.

STABILIZED WHIPPED CREAM USING UNFLAVORED GELATIN

All the above methods for stabilizing whipped cream are on the sweet side, if you'd like to have a sturdy cream that's less sweet, use the following recipe.

INGREDIENTS

- 1 cup heavy cream
- 2 tablespoons sugar
- 1 teaspoon pure vanilla extract
- 1 teaspoon unflavored gelatin
- 1-1/2 tablespoons water

INSTRUCTIONS

1. Use a microwave bowl, and sprinkle the gelatin over the water. Let it set for five minutes.
2. Microwave the gelatin for five to ten seconds until fully dissolved. No granules should be present. Check after five seconds, it may need a couple more seconds.
3. Combine heavy cream, sugar, and pure vanilla in a mixing bowl or standing mixer,
4. Beat until soft peaks form, and slowly add the gelatin.
5. Beat at high speed until stiff peaks form. When you raise your mixer, the peaks should form and not fall back into themselves when you hold your beaters upright.

CHEESECAKE TIPS

The ultimate smooth and creamy cheesecake can be difficult to achieve, but here are some tips to help you bake the best silky cheesecake. It is the method that matters.

- Softened cream cheese at room temperature is a must.
- Preheat the oven.
- Don't whip a lot of air into the batter. Mix the batter slowly.
- Fully incorporate the eggs one at a time.
- Use a piece of parchment paper on the bottom of the springform pan.
- Adding a little cornstarch or flour to the batter helps with cracking and stability.
- Tap the batter on the counter before putting it in the oven helps release air bubbles. Tap the batter in the bowl several times before adding it to the springform pan.
- Once the batter is in the springform pan, gently tap it on the counter again.
- Boil 4 to 6 cups of water. This will depend on the size of your roasting pan. Baking a cheesecake in a water bath and low and slow helps prevent cracking. The water bath also gives a creamy texture.
- Set the cheesecake pan in a slow cooker bag and twist together the sides to make it fit snugly and tuck it in or tie it off.
- Wrap a large piece of heavy-duty foil around the slow cooker bag up to the height of the pan and press it firmly to fit the pan. It must be one piece of foil.
- Put the cheesecake in the oven on a roasting pan.
- Carefully pour the water around the cheesecake.
- Bake 9" cheesecakes at 325 F degrees for 65-70 minutes or until the filling is almost set.
- Insert a thermometer into the center of the cheesecake. It should read 150 degrees.
- Pull the oven rack out slightly and run a knife or small offset spatula around the edge of the cake pan, preventing the cheesecake from sticking to the sides. As the cake cools, it will contract and pull away from the sides of the pan. If the cheesecake sticks to the edges, it will crack.
- Crack the oven and let the cheesecake remain in it for thirty minutes. Leaving the cheesecake in the oven when done with the oven off and the door cracked, helps prevent cracks but leaving it too long will dry it out.
- After a cheesecake is in the refrigerator all night, remove the side walls. Once removed from the pan, flip it over on a cake board. Run a sharp knife between the cheesecake and the bottom of the springform pan. Now, remove the pan and parchment paper. Flip the cheesecake back over on a plate or another cake board.
- Slice a cold cheesecake with a warmed chef's knife. Wipe the knife after each cut.

INTERNAL TEMPERATURE

How do you know if a dessert is done? The best way to tell if a cheesecake, pie, pudding, custard, cream anglaise/vanilla sauce, pastry cream, bread pudding, creme brulee, or even cake is done is to check the internal temperature. Use a fast and accurate instant-read thermometer. Checking the temperature will spare you a lot of dessert failures.

You'll find internal temperatures in my recipe instructions. Before you remove your dessert from the oven, check the internal temperature. It'll help you make a perfect winning dessert.

CREAMY APPLE DESSERTS
"The Beginning of a World Food Champion."

We all love apple desserts. They remind us of a favorite fall memory, like being at grandma's house eating a piece of her homemade apple pie.

Asking the question, "What is your favorite dessert?" is how I love to start conversations. Most people have a favorite dessert and get excited talking about it. The majority of the time, their favorite dessert is an apple-related dessert or a banana pudding attached to a favorite memory.

I have three apple desserts with rare perfect scores at the World Food Championships. They're not only full of flavor and taste fabulous, but they bring back exciting memories. Apple desserts are full of warm and cozy fall spices.

To increase the flavor, I toast the spices in a skillet before adding them to my dry ingredients. Toasting them awakens the lifeless spices, and brings out an even more beautiful aroma that awakens memories.

Maybe I'm being a little dramatic, but it is a chef's secret weapon and one I use often.

I have both a stove-top and a microwave version for making homemade caramel sauce and butterscotch sauce. During my food competitions, I have to find ways to cut time. Using my microwave for sauces saves time and is less likely to burn.

In a lot of my apple recipes, I include a crisp. There is little difference between a crisp and a crumble. A crisp includes oats which go perfectly with apples. You can't beat the texture oats add to an apple dessert which is why I use them.

If this is your first time making a pudding or vanilla cream sauce, I recommend cooking it over low heat or using a double boiler. You can also control the heat by pulling the pot off the heat and whisking well before returning it to the heat.

Many of my apple pie recipes include apple pie spice. You can make your own apple pie spice with the recipe below.

APPLE PIE SPICE

INGREDIENTS

- 2 tablespoons ground cinnamon
- 1 tablespoon ground nutmeg
- 1-1/2 teaspoons ground allspice
- 1-1/2 teaspoons ground cardamom
- ¼ teaspoon of ginger

TIP
Toast the spices in a skillet until they smell aromatic to increase the flavor.

APPLE CHEESECAKE PIE

With Crisp and Salted Caramel Sauce

You'll love the creaminess of a cheesecake with the apple pie filling. This apple cheesecake pie is elevated with a crunchy oat crisp. Even though this recipe has several layers, they're all easy to prepare. This pie is also elevated with a delicious homemade salted caramel sauce, but you can purchase a store-bought salted caramel ice cream topping.

APPLE PIE SPICED GRAHAM CRACKER CRUST

INGREDIENTS

- 1-1/2 cups graham cracker crumbs
- 6 tablespoons butter, melted
- ¼ cup brown sugar
- 1-1/2 teaspoon apple pie spice or cinnamon

INSTRUCTIONS

1. Place the graham crackers in a food processor and process until fine crumbs. You can also break up the sheets and place them in a ziplock bag. Use a mallet or rolling pin to crush the crackers into crumbs.
2. Add the melted butter, sugar, and apple pie spice to your crumbs and mix thoroughly.
3. Press over the bottom and sides of a 9-inch pie or tart pan.
4. Bake at 350 degrees for 10 minutes.
5. Cool completely before adding the cream cheese filling.

CREAM CHEESE FILLING

INGREDIENTS

- 1 cup heavy cream, whipped stiff
- 1 (8 ounces) of full-fat cream cheese
- 1 cup powdered sugar
- 2 teaspoons pure vanilla extract

INSTRUCTIONS

1. Whip the heavy cream with a half cup of powdered sugar on medium speed until stiff peaks, 3 to 5 minutes.
2. In a separate bowl, beat the cream cheese and the remaining half cup of powdered sugar on medium speed until creamy.
3. Scrape down the bowl again. Mix in the vanilla.
4. Using a rubber spatula, gently fold the whipped heavy cream into the cream cheese mixture.
5. Smooth out the creamy mixture in the pie crust.
6. Refrigerate for an hour.
7. Remove from the refrigerator, add the cooled apple pie filling on the cream cheese layer, and refrigerate.

APPLE PIE FILLING

INGREDIENTS

- 3 large apples peeled, cored, and diced into inch cubes (Gala or Cosmic Crisp)
- 1 tablespoon fresh lemon juice
- 2 tablespoons butter
- 2 tablespoons maple syrup
- 1 tablespoon flour
- 1/4 cup brown sugar, packed
- 1/4 cup granulated sugar
- 1/4 teaspoon salt
- 3/4 teaspoon ground cinnamon
- 1/8 teaspoon ground ginger
- 1/4 teaspoon nutmeg
- 1/4 teaspoon allspice
- 1 teaspoon pure vanilla extract

INSTRUCTIONS

1. In a medium saucepan, cook the following until the apples are fork-tender.
2. Peel, core, and chop the apples into an inch size.
3. In a large skillet on medium heat, stir together the apples, and lemon juice.
4. Stir in the butter and maple syrup until melted.
5. Add the flour, brown sugar, sugar, salt, cinnamon, ginger, nutmeg, and allspice.
6. Stick a knife or fork into an apple to check for tenderness.
7. When almost done, stir in the vanilla.
8. Spread the apples over a baking sheet to cool.
9. Cool completely before adding the apples on the cream cheese layer.

CRISP TOPPING

INGREDIENTS

- 1/2 cup all-purpose flour
- 1/2 cup rolled oats
- 1/2 cup brown sugar
- 1/2 cup pecans, finely chopped
- 1-½ teaspoon apple pie spice
- ¼ teaspoon salt
- 5 tablespoons butter, melted

INSTRUCTIONS

1. Whisk the flour, oats, brown sugar, pecans, apple pie spice, and salt.
2. Add the melted butter and maple syrup and stir using a rubber spatula.
3. The mixture should come together and be crumbly.
4. Spread the crumble out on a parchment-lined baking sheet pan.
5. Bake at 375 degrees for 10 minutes.
6. Using a metal spatula, stir the crumble and continue cooking for another 15 minutes or until golden brown.
7. Cool completely.
8. Spreading the crumble over the pie just before serving will keep it crunchy.

PLATING

Drizzle each slice of pie with salted caramel sauce.

SALTED CARAMEL SAUCE

INGREDIENTS

- 1 cup granulated sugar
- 2 tablespoons corn syrup
- 2 tablespoons water
- 1/2 cup heavy cream, lukewarm
- 4 tablespoons butter, cut into cubes
- 1/2 teaspoon salt
- 2 teaspoons pure vanilla extract

INSTRUCTIONS

1. Add the sugar, water, and corn syrup to a saucepan and combine well using a silicone spatula.
2. The sugar will dissolve but have clumps and be cloudy at first.
3. Do not stir while the sugar is cooking. Swirl the mixture in the saucepan.
4. Remove from the heat immediately at 330 F degrees, use a candy thermometer.
5. Stand back and reach to pour the lukewarm cream into the pot carefully. It will bubble up.
6. When the bubbles recede, stir well on low heat. If it clumps up, keep stirring over the low heat.
7. Add the butter, salt, and vanilla and combine.
8. Let the caramel cool.
9. It will thicken as it cools.

MICROWAVE INSTRUCTIONS

1. Mix the sugar, corn syrup, and water in a 4-cup microwave-safe measuring cup.
2. Microwave on full power for 5 - 7 minutes, depending on your microwave. The mixture should begin to turn brown.
3. Remove from the microwave and let it sit on the counter for 5 minutes. It will darken to a warm caramel color.
4. After the caramel darkens, stir in the warm cream, a little at a time so the caramel won't bubble up.
5. If you have lumps, return the caramel to the microwave for thirty seconds.
6. Add the butter, salt, and vanilla and stir until smooth.
7. Let the caramel cool.
8. It will thicken as it cools.

TIP

Turn this pie into elegant caramel apple layered desserts using small glasses, individual trifle bowls, or mason jars. Add a couple of tablespoons of graham cracker crust to the bottom of the glass. Fold ⅓ cup of caramel into the cheesecake layer. Continue layering the apple pie filling. Top with whipped cream and an elegant apple rose (See Page 27).

CREAMY APPLE TART

With Elegant Apple Rose Design

A version of this recipe earned a rare perfect score at the World Food Championships. It takes a little work and can't be made in advance, but perfect for a special occasion and so worth the extra effort.

TIP

For my perfect score dessert, Salted Caramel Sauce (See Page 28) and toasted salted pecans (See Page 64) was layered to the bottom of the crust before adding the pudding.

APPLE PIE SPICED GRAHAM CRACKER CRUST

INGREDIENTS

- 2 cups graham cracker crumbs
- 9 tablespoons butter, melted
- 1/3 cup brown sugar
- 1-1/2 teaspoons apple pie spice or cinnamon
- 1 – 10-inch tart pan

INSTRUCTIONS

1. Place the graham crackers in a food processor and process until fine crumbs. You can also break up the sheets and place them in a ziplock bag. Use a mallet or rolling pin to crush the crackers into crumbs.
2. Add the melted butter, sugar, and apple pie spice to your crumbs and mix thoroughly.
3. Press over the bottom and sides of the tart pan.
4. Bake at 350 degrees for 10 minutes.
5. Cool at room temperature before removing from the tart pan.

VANILLA PUDDING FILLING

INGREDIENTS

- 2 cups half-and-half
- 3/4 cup sugar
- 4 egg yolks
- 1/4 cup cornstarch
- 1/8 teaspoon salt
- 1 teaspoon vanilla paste
- 1 teaspoon apple pie spice
- 2 tablespoons butter
- ½ cup heavy cream

INSTRUCTIONS

1. Heat half-and-half and sugar in the microwave for about two to three minutes on full power. The half-and-half should be steaming but not boiling. Stir it well before and after heating. You can heat the milk on the stove, but it will burn and needs to be watched.
2. Whisk egg yolks until a pale-yellow color.
3. Whisk in cornstarch and salt with the egg yolks. Once the egg yolks and cornstarch are light and smooth, it is ready for the milk.
4. Temper Eggs: Place a silicone mat or a towel under your bowl to prevent it from slipping. Slowly drizzle a cup of warm milk over the egg mixture while constantly whisking. Use one hand to drizzle the milk into the egg yolks and one hand to whisk the mixture. Whisk in the remaining warm milk.
5. Pour the mixture into a clean pot and whisk over medium-low heat until it thickens.
6. Cook while whisking until the pudding is thick, about 175 F.-180 F. degrees.
7. Pull the pudding on and off the burner if needed to whisk. It should coat the back of a spoon. When you run your fingers through it, and it stays separated, it's ready.
8. Remove from the heat, add the butter, apple pie spice, and vanilla, and whisk until the butter melts and incorporates.
9. Place in a bowl, and cover with plastic wrap directly on the pudding to prevent skin from forming.
10. Let it cool completely at room temperature and refrigerate until thick.
11. Whip the ½ cup of heavy cream and fold it into the pudding.
12. Layer the pudding into the tart crust and refrigerate.

PUDDING TIPS

1. If this is your first time making pudding, I recommend cooking this sauce over low heat or using a double boiler. You can also control the heat by pulling the pot off the heat and whisking well before returning it to the heat.
2. It will thicken as it cools down. Whisk it well before using it.

MAPLE SPICED WHIPPED CREAM

INGREDIENTS

- 1 cup heavy whipping cream
- 1/2 cup powdered sugar
- 1 teaspoon pure vanilla extract
- 1/2 teaspoon cinnamon
- 4 ounces cream cheese, softened
- 2 tablespoons maple syrup

INSTRUCTIONS

1. Beat the heavy cream using an electric mixer until foamy. Gradually add the powdered sugar while continuing to beat.
2. Add the vanilla and cinnamon and beat until stiff peaks form.
3. In a separate bowl, combine the cream cheese and maple syrup until smooth.
4. Fold half a cup of the whipped cream into the cream cheese mixture to loosen it.
5. Fold the rest of the whipped cream into the cream cheese.
6. Spread the cream cheese whipped cream over the pudding layer.
7. Cover and refrigerate while cutting the apples.

APPLE ROSE DESIGN FOR TOP OF PIE

Apple roses are simple to make but a tedious procedure. The stunning presentation is worth the effort.

INGREDIENTS

- 3 large apples, cored and sliced (Gala, Honeycrisp, Cosmic)
- ½ cup orange juice
- 1/3 cup Orange marmalade

INSTRUCTIONS

1. Core the apples and slice them thin using a mandolin. You can use a knife and cut the apple slices about 1/8-inch thick.
2. Arrange the apple slices flat on a microwaveable plate. You will need several plates to cook all the apples.
3. Sprinkle the orange juice over the apple slices.
4. Microwave for one minute to soften the apples. Cook until limp. Too much heat will brown the apples. It will take two to three minutes. Check the apples after each minute.
5. Let the apples cool before drying them with paper towels.
6. Starting at the outer edge, arrange the apples in tight circles, overlapping each previous slice. Take care to make sure the colorful apple peel edges are pointing out. Keep adding slices of overlapping apples. Work your way to the center of the pie.
7. Roll up the last few slices into a tight circle and tuck it in the center of the apple rose.
8. Melt the orange marmalade in the microwave for 30 seconds or until melted.
9. Brush the apples with the marmalade. The jelly gives the apples a beautiful shine.
10. Best if eaten the same day it is made.

APPLE PIE CRISP

In Individual Puff Pastry with Crème Anglaise

Who doesn't love a flaky puff pastry? Store-bought puff pastry is a shortcut to making a homemade pie crust or even a cookie crust. The individual pie portions cook faster than a whole pie. Jumbo-size muffin tins were used in the recipe, but you can use regular muffin tins. This recipe was a hit on my easy recipe blog.

APPLE PIE FILLING

INGREDIENTS

- 8 medium apples peeled, cored, and diced into ½ inch pieces.
- ½ lemon, juiced
- 2 tablespoons flour
- ½ cup brown sugar, packed
- 1/2 cup granulated sugar
- 1/2 teaspoon salt
- 1-1/2 teaspoons ground cinnamon
- 1/4 teaspoon ground ginger
- 1/2 teaspoon nutmeg
- ½ teaspoon allspice

INSTRUCTIONS

1. Peel, core, and chop the apples into 1-inch pieces.
2. Stir the apples and lemon juice together.
3. Add the flour, brown sugar, sugar, salt, cinnamon, ginger, nutmeg, and allspice and combine.

CRISP

INGREDIENTS

- 1 cup all-purpose flour
- 1 cup rolled oats
- 1 cup brown sugar
- 2 teaspoon apple pie spice
- ¼ teaspoon salt
- 10 tablespoons butter, melted
- 1/2 cup pecans, finely chopped

INSTRUCTIONS

1. Whisk the flour, oats, brown sugar, apple pie spice, and salt.
2. Add the melted butter and stir using a rubber spatula.
3. Stir in the pecans.
4. The mixture should come together and be crumbly.

PUFF PASTRY

INGREDIENTS

- 1-box Puff Pastry (2 sheets)

INSTRUCTIONS

1. Prepare the pastry. You'll need both sheets.
2. Leave the puff pastry refrigerated until ready to roll out. The butter in the pastry needs to stay cold.
3. Cut each pastry into 6 equal parts for jumbo-size muffin tins.
4. Spray the muffin tin with cooking spray. Place the puff pastry squares into each muffin tin.
5. Divide the apple filling evenly into the individual puff pastry.
6. Divide the crumble evenly over the pie filling.
7. Bake at 375 degrees for 25 - 30 minutes until golden brown.
8. Drizzle with Salted Caramel Sauce and Cream Anglaise or serve with ice cream.

CREME ANGLAISE

Crème Anglaise, known as the vanilla cream sauce or anglaise, is a dessert sauce often served cold, but it's fabulous served warm over a piece of pie, cake, bread pudding, ice cream, and this puff pastry apple pie. It will remind you of melted ice cream, which is why it goes well with this apple pie.

INGREDIENTS

- 2 cups heavy cream
- 6 egg yolks, room temperature
- 1/2 cup sugar
- 1 tablespoon vanilla paste

INSTRUCTIONS

1. Combine the heavy cream and sugar in a microwave-safe bowl.
2. Heat for two to three minutes until steaming.
3. Whisk together the egg yolks until light.
4. Slowly drizzle one cup of warm milk into the eggs while whisking constantly. Add the rest of the milk.
5. Cook on the stovetop using medium heat, and stir constantly.
6. Remove it from the heat between 175 – 180 F. degrees.
7. Stir in the vanilla paste.
8. Strain for a smoother sauce.
9. Put plastic wrap on the surface and cool to room temperature.
10. Crème anglaise keeps in the refrigerator for up to three days.

TIPS

1. If this is your first time making a vanilla cream sauce, I recommend cooking this sauce over low heat or using a double boiler. You can also control the heat by pulling the pot off the heat and whisking well before returning it to the heat.
2. It will thicken as it cools down.

This delicious Crème Anglaise was served with my Apple Tart at the World Food Championships.

MINI APPLE CHEESECAKES
Butterscotch Sauce

Impress your guests with individual Apple Cheesecakes. If you have a mini cheesecake pan, use it. If not, simply use a regular-size muffin pan. Mini cheesecakes are easy to make. They do not require a springform pan or a water bath.

Butterscotch is a flavor that reminds me of my father. He loved it! Because he is no longer with us, I use it often in my desserts, especially apple dishes. This butterscotch apple cheesecake is creamy and double comforting with the apples and butterscotch. To make the sauce easier, I included a microwave version.

GRAHAM CRACKER CRUST

INGREDIENTS

- 1-1/2 cups graham cracker crumbs
- 7 tablespoons butter, melted
- 1/4 cup brown sugar
- 1-1/2 teaspoon apple pie spice or cinnamon

INSTRUCTIONS

1. Preheat the oven to 325 degrees F.
2. Use a 12-cup mini cheesecake pan with removable bottoms or regular muffin tin. Use cupcake liners with the muffin tin. Spray pans with baking spray.
3. Place the graham crackers in a food processor and process until fine crumbs or crush the crackers in a ziplock bag using a mallet or rolling pin.
4. Stir in the melted butter, sugar, and apple pie spice, and combine.
5. Evenly distribute the crumb mixture between the bottom of each cupcake liner and press down using a tablespoon or small glass.
6. Bake crust for 6 minutes.
7. Cool to room temperature.

CHEESECAKE FILLING

INGREDIENTS

- 2 (8-oz.) full-fat cream cheese, softened
- 3/4 cup sugar
- 1-1/2 teaspoons pure vanilla extract
- 2 large eggs
- 1/4 cup sour cream
- 2 tablespoons heavy cream

INSTRUCTIONS

1. Preheat oven 325-degree oven.
2. Whip the cream cheese, sugar, vanilla, and apple pie spice until fluffy. Beat for four to five minutes at low speed.
3. Mix in the eggs one at a time.
4. Keep the mixer low and add sour cream and heavy cream.
5. Scrape down the sides and bottom and blend.
6. Use an ice cream scoop and scoop even amounts of cheesecake filling on top of each graham cracker crust.
7. Place a 9x13 baking pan in the oven and pour the hot water into it.
8. Bake cheesecakes for 20 - 25 minutes until the filling is almost set. The center will jiggle slightly.
9. Remove from the oven and cool before placing in the refrigerator.

APPLE PIE FILLING

INGREDIENTS

- 3 large apples peeled, cored, and diced into ½-inch cubes
- Juice from half a lemon
- 2 tablespoons butter
- 1 tablespoon maple syrup
- 1 tablespoon flour
- 1/4 cup brown sugar, packed
- 1/4 cup granulated sugar
- 1/4 teaspoon salt
- 3/4 teaspoon ground cinnamon
- 1/8 teaspoon ground ginger
- 1/4 teaspoon nutmeg
- 1/4 teaspoon allspice
- 1 teaspoon pure vanilla extract

INSTRUCTIONS

1. In a medium saucepan, cook the following until the apples are fork-tender.
2. Peel, core, and chop the apples into an inch size.
3. In a large skillet on medium heat, stir together the apples, and lemon juice.
4. Stir in the butter and maple syrup until melted.
5. Add the flour, brown sugar, sugar, salt, cinnamon, ginger, nutmeg, and allspice.
6. Stick a knife or fork into an apple to check for tenderness.
7. When almost done, stir in the vanilla.
8. Spread the apples over a baking sheet to cool.
9. Cool completely before adding the apples on top of the cheesecake.

CRISP

INGREDIENTS

- 1/4 cup all-purpose flour
- 1/4 cup rolled oats
- 1/4 cup brown sugar
- 1/4 cup pecans, finely chopped
- 1/2 teaspoon apple pie spice
- ¼ teaspoon salt
- 3 tablespoons butter, melted

INSTRUCTIONS

1. Whisk the flour, oats, brown sugar, pecans, apple pie spice, and salt.
2. Add the melted butter and stir using a rubber spatula.
3. The mixture should come together and be crumbly.
4. Spread the crumble out on a parchment-lined baking sheet pan.
5. Bake at 375 degrees for 10 minutes.
6. Using a metal spatula, stir the crumble and continue cooking for another 10 minutes or until golden brown.
7. Cool completely and break up into tiny crumbs.
8. Spreading the crumble over the pie just before serving will keep it crunchy.

BUTTERSCOTCH SAUCE

INGREDIENTS

- 4 tablespoons butter
- 1 cup dark brown sugar
- ¾ cup heavy cream
- 2 teaspoons pure vanilla extract
- 1/2 teaspoon salt

INSTRUCTIONS

1. Melt the butter in a heavy saucepan.
2. Stir in the dark brown sugar and continue stirring until the sugar is moist.
3. Stop whisking and allow the mixture to boil for 4 - 5 minutes.
4. Add the heavy cream. Continue stirring until the mixture is smooth.
5. It should reach 225 F. degrees.
6. Remove from the heat and stir in the salt and vanilla.
7. Cool slightly and put into a mason jar. Cool completely and refrigerate.
8. Butterscotch thickens as it cools.

MICROWAVE INSTRUCTIONS

1. Melt the butter in a 4-cup microwave measuring cup for one minute.
2. Stir in the dark brown sugar and mix well.
3. Add the heavy cream to the brown sugar and combine.
4. Microwave for two-three minutes or until the mixture is bubbly. It should be 225 degrees.
5. Carefully remove the butterscotch from the microwave.
6. Stir in the salt and vanilla.
7. Cool slightly and put into a mason jar. Cool completely and refrigerate.
8. Butterscotch thickens as it cools.

SPICE WHIPPED CREAM

INGREDIENTS

- 1 cup heavy whipping cream
- 1/3 cup powdered sugar
- 1/2 teaspoon apple pie spice

INSTRUCTIONS

1. Beat heavy cream at high speed using an electric mixer until foamy. Gradually add the powdered sugar while continuing to beat.
2. Add the apple pie spice and beat until stiff peaks.

PLATING

1. Take the paper off the cheesecakes and place it on the plate.
2. Add a tablespoon of apple pie filling to the cheesecake.
3. Sprinkle the crisp over the apple pie filling.
4. Drizzle the plate and cheesecake with butterscotch.
5. Pipe homemade spiced whipped cream beside the cheesecakes.

APPLE PIE COOKIE CUPS

One of my earlier tips was to include something crunchy in your desserts. You can't get better than a crunchy cookie. Brush melted caramel chips in the bottom of these cookie cups. It acts as a layer of protection from the pudding. Cut the apple pieces small and the same size so the apples will cook evenly and quickly.

COOKIE CUPS

INGREDIENTS

- 1 cup butter, softened
- 1-1/2 cups sugar
- 2 eggs
- 3 teaspoons pure vanilla extract
- 2-3/4 cups of all-purpose flour
- 1 teaspoon baking powder
- 1 teaspoon salt
- ½ cup caramel chips

INSTRUCTIONS

1. Preheat oven to 350 degrees. Spray two regular-size muffin tins with cooking spray.
2. Cream the butter and sugar until fluffy using a mixer.
3. Add eggs one at a time and continue beating until incorporated.
4. Mix in the vanilla.
5. Whisk the flour, baking powder, and salt together.
6. Add the dry ingredients to the butter, sugar, and egg mixture until combined.
7. Use a regular ice cream scoop (3 tablespoons), and scoop dough into muffin tins.
8. Bake for 12 minutes. The edges will be slightly golden.
9. Remove the cookie cups from the oven.
10. Use a tablespoon or a small round lid to press an indention in the middle of the hot cookie.
11. Melt the caramel chips in the microwave for 30 seconds and stir until smooth.
12. Brush the inside of each warm cookie with melted caramel chips.
13. Cool for ten minutes in the pan.
14. Remove from the pan and place on a large baking sheet.
15. Cool completely.

APPLE PIE FILLING

INGREDIENTS

- 3 large apples peeled, cored, and diced into ½-inch cubes
- Juice from half a lemon
- 2 tablespoons butter
- 2 tablespoons maple syrup
- 1 tablespoon flour
- 1/4 cup brown sugar, packed
- 1/4 cup granulated sugar
- 1/4 teaspoon salt
- 3/4 teaspoon ground cinnamon
- 1/8 teaspoon ground ginger
- 1/4 teaspoon nutmeg
- 1/4 teaspoon allspice
- 1 teaspoon pure vanilla extract

INSTRUCTIONS

1. In a medium saucepan, cook the following until the apples are fork-tender.
2. Peel, core, and chop the apples into an inch size.
3. In a large skillet, stir the apples and lemon juice on medium heat.
4. Stir in the butter and maple syrup until melted.
5. Add the flour, brown sugar, sugar, salt, cinnamon, ginger, nutmeg, and allspice.
6. Stick a knife or fork into an apple to check for tenderness.
7. When almost done, stir in the vanilla.
8. Spread the apples over a baking sheet to cool.
9. Cool completely before adding the apples to the cookie cups.

APPLE PIE SPICED WHIPPED CREAM

INGREDIENTS

- 1-1/2 cups heavy whipping cream, cold
- 1/2 cup confectioners' sugar
- 3/4 teaspoon apple pie spice

INSTRUCTIONS

1. Beat heavy cream using an electric mixer until foamy. Gradually add the powdered sugar and apple pie spice while beating until stiff peaks.

ASSEMBLE THE APPLE PIE COOKIE CUPS

1. Fill the cookie cups with the apple pie filling.
2. Pipe the spice whipped cream on each cookie.

FLAKY APPLE TURNOVER
With Maple Glaze

These apple turnovers are perfect for dessert or even breakfast. They are so flakey using puff pastry. Cut the apple pieces small and the same size so the apples will cook evenly and quickly.
1 (7-1/4 ounce box) frozen puffed pastry, thaw in the refrigerator

APPLE PIE FILLING

The apple pieces need to be small due to the short baking time.

INGREDIENTS

- 3 large apples peeled, cored, and diced into ½-inch cubes
- Juice from 1/2 lemon
- 2 tablespoons maple syrup
- 1 tablespoon flour
- 1/4 cup brown sugar, packed
- 1/4 cup granulated sugar
- 1/4 teaspoon salt
- 3/4 teaspoon ground cinnamon
- 1/8 teaspoon ground ginger
- 1/4 teaspoon nutmeg
- 1/4 teaspoon allspice
- 1 teaspoon pure vanilla extract
- 1 (7-1/4 ounce box) frozen puffed pastry, thaw in the refrigerator

INSTRUCTIONS

1. Peel, core, and chop the apples into ½ inch size.
2. Stir together the apples and the lemon juice.
3. Mix in the maple syrup.
4. Add the flour, brown sugar, sugar, salt, cinnamon, ginger, nutmeg, allspice, and vanilla.
5. Divide between pastries.

PASTRY INSTRUCTIONS

1. Follow the package instructions for thawing.
2. Preheat the oven to 400 F. degrees.
3. Separate the puff pastry sheets.
4. Cut each pastry sheet into four squares.
5. Divide the pie filling evenly between the eight pastry squares.
6. Brush the edges with water.
7. Fold them over diagonally.
8. Seal them with a fork.
9. Use a knife and make a small slit on the top of the pastry.
10. Bake on parchment paper at 400 degrees for 20 minutes or until the tops are golden.

MAPLE GLAZE

INGREDIENTS

- 3 tablespoons butter
- 1/3 cup pure maple syrup
- 1 teaspoon pure vanilla
- ½ teaspoon maple extract
- ¼ teaspoon salt
- 1-½ cups powdered sugar

INSTRUCTIONS

1. Melt the butter in a saucepan over medium heat.
2. Whisk in the maple syrup.
3. Stir in the vanilla, maple extract, and salt.
4. Remove from heat and whisk in the powdered sugar a little at a time.
5. Dip or drizzle the glaze over the apple turnovers.

EASY APPLE BUTTERSCOTCH CRISP

Do you have plenty of apples or a crowd to feed? Whip up this quick and easy apple crisp. Serve with homemade butterscotch sauce and some ice cream. You'll be the hit of the party.

TIPS

Put your butterscotch sauce in a mason jar. It travels well. You can microwave it, before pouring it over a dessert. Cut the apple pieces small and the same size so the apples will cook evenly and quickly.

APPLE PIE FILLING

INGREDIENTS

- 8 medium apples peeled, cored, and diced into inch cubes.
- Juice from one lemon
- 2 tablespoons flour
- ½ cup brown sugar, packed
- 1/2 cup granulated sugar
- 1/2 teaspoon salt
- 1-1/2 teaspoons ground cinnamon
- 1/4 teaspoon ground ginger
- 1/2 teaspoon nutmeg
- ½ teaspoon allspice
- 2 teaspoons pure vanilla extract
- 1 cup butterscotch chips

INSTRUCTIONS

1. Peel, core, and chop the apples into ½ inch size.
2. Stir together the apples and the lemon juice.
3. Add the flour, brown sugar, sugar, salt, cinnamon, ginger, nutmeg, allspice, and vanilla.
4. Mix well and place into a 9 x 13 baking dish sprayed with cooking spray.
5. Sprinkle the butterscotch chips over the apples.

BUTTERSCOTCH CRISP

INGREDIENTS

- 1 cup all-purpose flour
- 1 cup rolled oats
- 1 cup brown sugar
- 2 teaspoons apple pie spice
- ¼ teaspoon salt
- 10 tablespoons butter, melted
- 1/2 cup pecans, finely chopped
- 1 cup butterscotch chips

INSTRUCTIONS

1. Whisk the flour, oats, brown sugar, apple pie spice, and salt.
2. Add the melted butter and stir using a rubber spatula.
3. Stir in the pecans and butterscotch chips.
4. The mixture should come together and be crumbly.
5. Divide the crumble evenly over the pie filling.
6. Bake for 45 minutes until the apples are tender and the crumble is golden brown.
7. Serve with vanilla ice cream and butterscotch sauce.

BUTTERSCOTCH SAUCE

INGREDIENTS

- 4 tablespoons butter
- 1 cup dark brown sugar
- ¾ cup heavy cream
- 2 teaspoons pure vanilla extract
- 1/2 teaspoon salt

INSTRUCTIONS

1. Melt the butter in a heavy saucepan.
2. Stir in the dark brown sugar and continue stirring until the sugar is moistened.
3. Stop whisking and allow the mixture to boil for 4 - 5 minutes.
4. Add the heavy cream. Continue stirring until the mixture is smooth.
5. It should reach 225 F. degrees.
6. Remove from the heat and stir in the salt and vanilla.
7. Cool slightly and put into a mason jar. Cool completely and refrigerate.
8. Butterscotch thickens as it cools.
9. Microwave the sauce in the mason jar before drizzling it over apple crisp.

APPLE HAND PIES

With Maple Caramel Glaze

I started making hand pies during Covid when making individual desserts was considered "safer." They were cute and delicious. Homemade apple pie filling and crust are the two main ingredients. Nothing is better than individual apple pies. After all, apple pie is the all-American dessert.
Pie Crust Recipe. (See Page 13) Cut the apple pieces small and the same size so the apples will cook evenly and quickly.

APPLE PIE FILLING

INGREDIENTS

- 3 large apples peeled, cored, and diced into ½-inch cubes
- Juice from half a lemon
- 1 tablespoon flour
- 1/4 cup brown sugar, packed
- 1/4 cup granulated sugar
- 1/4 teaspoon salt
- 3/4 teaspoon ground cinnamon
- 1/8 teaspoon ground ginger
- 1/4 teaspoon nutmeg
- 1/4 teaspoon allspice
- 1 teaspoon pure vanilla extract

INSTRUCTIONS

1. In a medium saucepan, cook the following until the apples are fork-tender.
2. Peel, core, and chop the apples into ½ inch size.
3. In a large skillet on medium heat, stir the apples and lemon juice.
4. Add the flour, brown sugar, sugar, salt, cinnamon, ginger, nutmeg, allspice, and vanilla.
5. Stick a knife or fork into an apple to check for tenderness.
6. Cool completely.
7. Divide between pastries.

CRUST

INGREDIENTS

- Double pie crust recipe (See Page 14)
- 2 large eggs are beaten with two tablespoons of milk.

INSTRUCTIONS

1. Roll out the dough until it is about ⅛ to ¼ inch thick.
2. Cut the dough into a circle using a five-inch round cookie cutter.
3. Add one heaping tablespoon of filling to the center.
4. Fold the dough in half and use a fork to crimp the edges.
5. Place hand pies on a baking sheet lined with parchment paper.
6. In a small bowl, whisk together the egg and milk.
7. Use a pastry brush to brush the pies with the egg wash.
8. Use a sharp knife tip and cut a small slit on the top of each pie.
9. Bake in a preheated 400-degree oven for 20 minutes or until golden brown.

MAPLE GLAZE

INGREDIENTS

- 3 tablespoons butter
- 1/3 cup pure maple syrup
- 1 teaspoon pure vanilla
- ½ teaspoon maple extract
- ¼ teaspoon salt
- 1-½ cups powdered sugar

INSTRUCTIONS

1. Melt the butter over medium heat.
2. Whisk in the maple syrup.
3. Stir in the vanilla, maple extract, and salt.
4. Remove from heat and whisk in the powdered sugar a little at a time.
5. Dip or drizzle apple turnovers.
6. Dust with cinnamon. (optional)
7. It will thicken as it cools.

TIP

Add a tablespoon of maple syrup if the glaze becomes too thick.

EXCELLENT EGG CUSTARD PIE

With Apple Spice Whipped Cream

Egg custard pie is an old fashion Southern treat. It is a cousin to a creme brulee with similar ingredients, milk, sugar, eggs, and vanilla. The egg custard pie is easier to make and doesn't have that hard sugar topping on a creme brulee. Both include a thick, rich, silky custard which is fabulous and comforting. Apple pie spice whipped cream is a perfect complement to this creamy pie.

EGG CUSTARD

INGREDIENTS

- ¼ cup butter
- 1 cup sugar
- ¼ teaspoon salt
- 4 eggs
- 2 teaspoons pure vanilla bean paste
- 3 cups half-and-half
- 9-inch pie crust, partially baked
- ½ teaspoon nutmeg

INSTRUCTIONS

1. Using an electric mixer, beat butter, sugar, and salt.
2. Add eggs slowly, one at a time beating until light.
3. Blend in half-and-half and vanilla.
4. Bake the pie crust for 10 minutes before adding the filling.
5. Pour in partially baked pie crust.
6. Lightly dust the top with nutmeg. Do not skip the nutmeg.
7. Bake at 350 F. degrees for 50-60 minutes until the filling sets.
8. The internal temperature should read 180 F. degrees on an instant-read thermometer inserted in the center.
9. Serve with Salted Caramel Sauce and Apple Pie Spice Whipped Cream.

APPLE PIE SPICED WHIPPED CREAM

INGREDIENTS

- 1-1/2 cups heavy whipped cream, cold
- 1/2 cup confectioners' sugar
- 1 teaspoon apple pie spice

INSTRUCTIONS

1. Beat heavy cream using an electric mixer until foamy. Gradually add the confectioners' sugar and apple pie spice while beating until stiff peaks.

CREAMY CHEESECAKE

Stacked with Apple Butterscotch Blondies and Butterscotch Sauce

I mentioned that I love big, eye-catching desserts. This cheesecake covered with moist apple blondies and butterscotch sauce is fabulous, and a must-have centerpiece for any special occasion. It takes a couple of days to prepare. The cheesecake needs to be refrigerated overnight before stacking the blondies on it.

Cheesecakes include simple ingredients. It's the method that matters most when baking a cheesecake to achieve a silky dessert. You can achieve the perfect cheesecake with the following tips, including checking the internal temperature of the cheesecake.

GRAHAM CRACKER CRUST

INGREDIENTS

- 2 cups graham cracker crumbs
- 9 tablespoons butter, melted
- 1/3 cup brown sugar
- 1-1/2 teaspoon cinnamon

INSTRUCTIONS

1. Preheat the oven to 325 F. degrees.
2. Combine graham cracker crumbs, melted butter, brown sugar, and cinnamon.
3. Press firmly over the bottom of a 9-inch or 10-inch springform pan with sides at least 3" inches tall.
4. Bake for 10 minutes.

CHEESECAKE FILLING

INGREDIENTS

- 4 (8-oz.) full-fat cream cheese, softened
- 1-1/2 cup sugar
- 2 tablespoons cornstarch
- 1 tablespoon pure vanilla paste
- 4 large eggs
- 1/2 cup sour cream
- ¼ cup heavy cream

INSTRUCTIONS

1. Preheat oven to 325 degrees.
2. Boil a kettle of water.
3. Using an electric mixer, whip the cream cheese until smooth.
4. Slowly drizzle in the sugar and mix until combined.
5. Add the cornstarch and vanilla.
6. Mix in the eggs one at a time until just combined.
7. Stir in the sour cream and heavy cream and mix until combined. Don't over-mix.
8. Tap the mixing bowl on the counter several times to release air bubbles.
9. The amount of water will depend on the size of your roasting pan.
10. Spread the cheesecake batter in the springform pan.
11. Set the cheesecake pan in a slow cooker bag and twist together the sides to make it fit snugly and tuck it in or tie it off.
12. Wrap a large piece of heavy-duty foil around the slow cooker bag up to the height of the pan and press it firmly to fit the pan.
13. Put the cheesecake in the oven on a roasting pan.
14. Carefully pour the hot water around the cheesecake.
15. Bake cheesecakes for 70-75 minutes or until the filling is almost set.
16. Insert a thermometer into the center of the cheesecake. It should read 150 degrees.
17. Leave your cheesecake in the oven and run a knife or small offset spatula around the edge of the cake pan, preventing the cheesecake from sticking to the sides. As the cake cools, it will contract and pull away from the sides of the pan. If the cheesecake sticks to the edges, it will crack.
18. Crack the oven and let the cheesecake remain in it for thirty minutes. Leaving the cheesecake in the oven with the oven off and the door cracked helps prevent cracks but leaving it too long will dry it out.
19. After a cheesecake is in the refrigerator all night, remove the side walls. Once removed from the pan, flip it over on a cake board. Run a sharp knife between the cheesecake and the bottom of the springform pan. Now, remove the pan and parchment paper. Flip the cheesecake back over on a plate or another cake board.
20. Slice a cold cheesecake with a warmed chef's knife. Wipe the knife clean after each cut.

APPLE BUTTERSCOTCH BLONDIES

INGREDIENTS

- 1 cup butter
- 2-1/2 cups brown sugar
- 1 tablespoon pure vanilla
- 2 teaspoons maple extract
- 3 large eggs
- 1 large apple, Gala
- 1-½ cups butterscotch chips
- 3 cups all-purpose flour (sift before measuring or weigh 390 grams)
- ½ teaspoon salt
- 2-½ teaspoons baking powder
- 1 teaspoon cinnamon

INSTRUCTIONS

1. Preheat the oven to 350 F. degrees.
2. In a large microwave-safe bowl, add the butter.
3. Cook for four minutes in the microwave until beginning to turn brown. Add another minute if necessary.
4. Using a silicone spatula, stir in the brown sugar and let cool.
5. Add the vanilla and maple extract. Mix well with an electric mixer.
6. Add the eggs one at a time after the sugar cools. Combine each egg before adding the next one.
7. Chop the apples into ½ inch pieces.
8. Stir the apples and butterscotch chips in the blondie batter.
9. Whisk the flour, salt, baking powder, and cinnamon in a separate bowl.
10. Slowly add the dry ingredients until well blended with the mixer on low. The batter will be thick.
11. Bake for 45 minutes. Insert a toothpick in the center. It will have crumbs on it but no liquid.
12. The internal temperature should be around 170 F. degrees.
13. Cool completely before cutting.

BUTTERSCOTCH SAUCE

INGREDIENTS

- 4 tablespoons butter
- 1 cup dark brown sugar
- ¾ cup heavy cream
- 2 teaspoons pure vanilla extract
- 1/2 teaspoon salt

INSTRUCTIONS

1. Melt the butter in a heavy saucepan.
2. Stir in the dark brown sugar and continue stirring until the sugar is moistened.
3. Stop whisking and allow the mixture to boil for 4 - 5 minutes.
4. Add the heavy cream. Continue stirring until the mixture is smooth.
5. It should reach 225 F. degrees.
6. Remove from the heat and stir in the salt and vanilla.
7. Cool slightly and put into a mason jar. Cool completely and refrigerate.
8. Butterscotch thickens as it cools.

LAYER THE CHEESECAKE

1. After refrigerating overnight, remove the pan and parchment paper.
2. Add a thin layer of butterscotch sauce.
3. Stack the blondies on the cheesecake.
4. Drizzle the room-temperature butterscotch sauce over the cheesecake and blondies. Using a piping page with a small hole cut out is less messy.
5. Refrigerate the cheesecake.

BANANA CREAM DESSERTS

Banana Pudding, Nanner Puddin', A Favorite Southern Dessert

Who doesn't love banana pudding? It's the most requested dessert in my family. It's a light, creamy treat perfect for any celebration or event. In this chapter, you'll find easy-to-make and made-from-scratch banana puddings. I entered one of the recipes in the National Banana Pudding Contest.
These puddings are beautiful in a large trifle bowl, but you can create elegant portions in mason jars, glasses, or small trifle dishes. The individual containers are perfect for a dinner party.
Another option to impress your guests is individual Banana Pudding Cheesecakes. If you have a mini cheesecake pan, use it. If not, simply use a regular-size muffin pan.
The last two recipes in this chapter include cake and banana pudding which are the perfect combination. You'll find an easy-to-make and a made-from-scratch version of a Banana Pudding Cake.

EASY BANANA CREAM TOFFEE PIE

VANILLA WAFER CRUST

INGREDIENTS

- 1-1/2 cups Vanilla Wafer crumbs
- 1/4 cup brown sugar
- 6 tablespoons butter, melted
- 1 teaspoon cinnamon

INSTRUCTIONS

1. Crush the Vanilla Wafers in a ziplock bag or a food processor into fine crumbs.
2. Transfer crumbs to a bowl and stir in sugar, butter, and cinnamon.
3. Press in the bottom and up the sides of a deep-dish pie plate. The filling makes a very tall pie. Use a deep-dish pie plate.
4. Bake at 350 degrees for 12 minutes.   Completely cool.

BANANA PUDDING

INGREDIENTS

- 2 cups whole milk
- 2 (3.4-ounce) boxes of instant banana pudding or vanilla pudding
- 8 ounces of cream cheese, softened
- 1 (14-ounce) can sweetened condensed milk
- 1 teaspoon pure vanilla extract
- 12-ounce container of frozen whipped topping, thawed
- 3 bananas, sliced and drizzled with lemon juice
- 1 cup toffee bits

INSTRUCTIONS

1. Whisk the instant pudding with milk until blended.
2. In a separate bowl, beat the cream cheese, sweetened condensed milk, and vanilla until smooth.
3. Stir the pudding into the cream cheese mixture once the pudding sets.
4. Fold two cups of the whipped topping into the pudding and cream cheese mixture.
5. Slice bananas and drizzle them with lemon juice.
6. Place the bananas in the bottom of the prebaked pie crust.
7. Pile the pudding over the bananas. It will be high.
8. Add the remaining whipped cream over the pudding and refrigerate for four hours.
9. Topping the pie with toffee bits and vanilla wafers just before serving will keep it fresh.

When plating, add salted caramel in the center of the plate and top with a piece of the pie.

MADE FROM SCRATCH BANANA CREAM PIE
With Salted Caramel

VANILLA WAFER CRUST

INGREDIENTS

- 1-1/2 cups Vanilla Wafer crumbs
- 1/4 cup brown sugar
- 6 tablespoons butter, melted
- 1 teaspoon cinnamon

INSTRUCTIONS

1. Crush the Vanilla Wafers in a ziplock bag or a food processor into fine crumbs.
2. Transfer crumbs to a bowl and stir in sugar, butter, and cinnamon.
3. Press in the bottom and up the sides of a deep-dish pie plate.
4. Bake at 350 degrees for 12 minutes. Completely cool.

BANANA CREAM

INGREDIENTS

- 2 cups half-and-half
- ½ banana
- 3/4 cup sugar
- 4 egg yolks
- 1/4 cup cornstarch
- 1/8 teaspoon salt
- 1 teaspoon pure vanilla extract
- 1 teaspoon of banana extract
- 2 tablespoons butter
- ½ cup salted pecans, chopped
- 3 bananas, sliced and drizzled with lemon juice

INSTRUCTIONS

1. Use a blender to combine the half-and-half and ½ banana until smooth.
2. Heat half-and-half, banana, and sugar in the microwave for about three to four minutes on full power. The half-and-half should be steaming but not boiling. Stir it well before and after heating. You can heat the milk on the stove, but it will burn and needs to be watched.
3. In a medium bowl, whisk egg yolks until a pale-yellow color.
4. Whisk in cornstarch and salt with the egg yolks. Once the egg yolks and cornstarch are light and smooth, it's ready for the warm half-and-half.
5. Temper Eggs: Place a silicone mat or a towel under your bowl to prevent it from slipping. Slowly drizzle a cup of warm half-and-half over the egg mixture while constantly whisking. Use one hand to drizzle the milk into the egg yolks and one hand to whisk the mixture. Whisk in the remaining warm milk.
6. Pour the mixture into a clean pot and whisk over medium-low heat until it thickens.
7. Cook while whisking until the pudding is thick, about 175 F. - 180 F. degrees.
8. Pull the pudding on and off the burner to whisk. It should coat the back of a spoon. When you run your fingers through it, it should remain separated.
9. Remove from the heat, add the butter, banana extract, and vanilla, and whisk until the butter melts and incorporates.
10. Place in a bowl and cover with plastic wrap directly on the pudding to prevent skin from forming.
11. Cool at room temperature.
12. Place in the refrigerator until firm for a couple of hours.
13. When ready to layer, whip the heavy cream.

LAYER THE BANANA PUDDING PIE

1. Slice bananas and lightly drizzle them with lemon juice.
2. Place the bananas in the bottom of the pre-baked and cooled pie crust.
3. Fold a 3/4 cup of the whipped cream into the pudding.
4. Layer the pudding in the pie crust.
5. Pipe or mound the remaining whipped cream over the pudding and refrigerate.
6. When plating, add salted caramel in the center of the plate and top with a piece of the pie. Garnish with slices of banana, salted pecans, and a Vanilla Wafer.

TIP

Use a 1M piping tip. Place the tip on the outside edge of the pie. Bring the pastry tip up and around, making a complete circle. Continue with the circle around the pie. Each circle will stand up against the previous one.

WHIPPED CREAM

INGREDIENTS

- 1-1/2 cup heavy whipping cream
- 3/4 cup powdered sugar
- 1 teaspoon pure vanilla extract
- 1 teaspoon banana extract

INSTRUCTIONS

1. Beat whipped cream at medium speed using an electric mixer until soft peaks form.
2. Slowly add the powdered sugar while continuing to beat.
3. Add the pure vanilla extract and banana extract, and beat until stiff peaks form.

TOASTED SALTED PECANS

INGREDIENTS

- 1 cups pecans, chopped
- 2 tablespoons butter
- 3/4 teaspoon fine sea salt

INSTRUCTIONS

1. In a small skillet, melt the butter and add the pecans. Sprinkle with salt. Toast until lightly tan and it has a nutty aroma. Let the pecans completely cool.

SALTED CARAMEL SAUCE

INGREDIENTS

- 1 cup granulated sugar
- 2 tablespoons corn syrup
- 2 tablespoons water
- 1/2 cup heavy cream, lukewarm
- 4 tablespoons butter, cut into cubes
- 1/2 teaspoon salt
- 2 teaspoons pure vanilla extract

INSTRUCTIONS

1. Add the sugar, water, and corn syrup to a saucepan and combine well using a silicone spatula.
2. The sugar will dissolve. At first, it will have clumps and be cloudy.
3. Do not stir while the sugar is cooking. Swirl the mixture in the saucepan.
4. Remove from the heat immediately at 330 F degrees, use a candy thermometer.
5. Stand back and reach to pour the lukewarm cream into the pot carefully. It will bubble up.
6. When the bubbles recede, stir well on low heat. If it clumps up, keep stirring over the low heat.
7. Add the butter, salt, and vanilla and combine.
8. Let the caramel cool.
9. It will thicken as it cools.

MICROWAVE INSTRUCTIONS FOR SALTED CARAMEL SAUCE

Homemade caramel includes simple ingredients but can be tricky to make. The sugar can quickly burn. It can boil over after adding the heavy cream which is why cooks don't like making caramel from scratch. If that is you, try making caramel sauce in your microwave.

INSTRUCTIONS

1. Mix the sugar, corn syrup, and water in a 4-cup microwave-safe measuring cup.
2. Microwave on full power for 5 - 7 minutes, depending on your microwave. The mixture should begin to turn brown.
3. Remove from the microwave and let it sit on the counter for 5 minutes. It will darken to a warm caramel color.
4. After the caramel darkens, stir in the warm cream a little at a time which helps the caramel from bubbling over.
5. If you have lumps, return the caramel to the microwave for thirty seconds.
6. Add the butter, salt, and vanilla and stir until smooth.

65

EASY BANANA PUDDING
With Vanilla Crunchies

PUDDING

INGREDIENTS

- 2 (3.4-ounce) boxes of instant banana pudding or vanilla pudding
- 3 cups whole milk
- 1 (8-ounce) cream cheese, softened
- 1 (14-ounce) sweetened condensed milk
- 1 teaspoon pure vanilla extract
- 12-ounce container of frozen whipped topping thawed
- 6 bananas, sliced and drizzled with lemon juice
- Vanilla Wafer Crunchies, recipe below

INSTRUCTIONS

1. Whisk the instant pudding with milk until blended.
2. In a separate bowl, beat the cream cheese, sweetened condensed milk, and vanilla until smooth.
3. Mix the pudding into the cream cheese mixture once the pudding sets.
4. Fold two cups of the whipped topping into the pudding and cream cheese mixture.
5. Slice bananas and lightly drizzle them with lemon juice.

VANILLA CRUNCHIES

INGREDIENTS

- 2 cups crushed Vanilla Wafer cookies
- 1 cup pecans, finely chopped
- 1/3 cup brown sugar
- 11 tablespoons butter, melted
- 1-1/2 teaspoons cinnamon

INSTRUCTIONS

1. Crush the Vanilla Wafers in a ziplock bag or a food processor.
2. Transfer crumbs to a bowl and stir in pecans, sugar, butter, and cinnamon.
3. Spread out on a large baking sheet.
4. Bake at 350 degrees for 10 minutes and stir.
5. Continue baking for about five minutes until golden.
6. Cool completely and break into pieces.

TIP
You can replace the crunchies with Vanilla Wafers, but they get soggy faster.

LAYER THE BANANA PUDDING

You'll need 6 Bananas

1. Slice bananas and lightly drizzle them with lemon juice.
2. Add 1/2 of the pudding mixture to the bottom of a 9 x 3 dish.
3. Followed by 1/2 of the Crunchies or Vanilla Wafers, 1/2 of the sliced bananas, and repeat.
4. Mound the remaining whipped topping on top and refrigerate for two to four hours.
5. Garnish with sliced bananas and Vanilla Wafers, when ready to serve.

TIP

Layer the banana pudding in individual glasses for a beautiful presentation.

MADE FROM SCRATCH
Banana Pudding

VANILLA CRUNCHIES

INGREDIENTS

- 2 cups crushed Vanilla Wafer cookie crumbs
- 1 cup pecans, finely chopped
- 1/3 cup brown sugar
- 11 tablespoons butter, melted
- 1-1/2 teaspoons cinnamon

INSTRUCTIONS

1. Crush the Vanilla Wafers in a ziplock bag or a food processor.
2. Transfer crumbs to a bowl and stir in pecans, sugar, butter, and cinnamon.
3. Spread out on a large baking sheet.
4. Bake at 350 degrees for 15 minutes. Cool completely and break into pieces.

TIP

You can replace the crunchies with Vanilla Wafers, but they get soggy faster.

MADE-FROM-SCRATCH BANANA PUDDING

INGREDIENTS

- 4 cups half-and-half
- 1 whole banana
- 1-1/2 cups sugar
- 1 whole banana
- 6 egg yolks
- 1/3 cup cornstarch
- 1/4 teaspoon salt
- 1 teaspoon of banana extract
- 4 tablespoons butter, sliced
- 2 teaspoon vanilla paste
- 5 bananas, sliced
- Homemade whipped cream
- Vanilla Wafer Crunchies
- Plus, 1 box of vanilla wafers

INSTRUCTIONS

1. Use a blender to combine the half-and-half and a whole banana until smooth.
2. Heat half-and-half, banana, and sugar in the microwave for about three to four minutes on full power. The half-and-half should be steaming but not boiling. Stir it well before and after heating. You can heat the milk on the stove, but it will burn and needs to be watched.
3. Whisk egg yolks until a pale-yellow color. Whisk in cornstarch and salt with the egg yolks. Once the egg yolks and cornstarch are light and smooth, it's ready for the milk.
4. Temper Eggs: Place a silicone mat or a towel under your bowl to prevent it from slipping. Slowly drizzle a cup of warm milk over the egg mixture while constantly whisking. Use one hand to drizzle the half-and-half into the egg yolks and one hand to whisk the mixture. Whisk in the remaining warm milk.
5. Pour the mixture into a clean pot and whisk over medium-low heat until it thickens.
6. Cook while whisking until the pudding is thick, about 175 F. - 180 F. degrees.
7. Pull the pudding on and off the burner if needed to whisk. It should coat the back of a spoon. When you run your fingers through it, and the pudding doesn't meet, it's ready.
8. Remove from the heat, add the butter, banana extract, and vanilla, and whisk until the butter melts and incorporates.
9. Place it in a bowl, and cover it with plastic wrap directly on the pudding to prevent skin from forming.
10. Cool at room temperature.
11. Place in the refrigerator until firm for a couple of hours.
12. Whip the heavy cream and fold two cups into the pudding.

WHIPPED CREAM

INGREDIENTS

- 1-1/2 cup heavy whipping cream
- 3/4 cup powdered sugar
- 1-1/2 teaspoon pure vanilla extract

INSTRUCTIONS

1. Beat whipped cream at medium speed using an electric mixer until foamy.
2. Slowly add the powdered sugar while continuing to beat.
3. Add the vanilla and beat until stiff peaks form.

LAYER THE BANANA PUDDING

1. Slice the five bananas and lightly drizzle them with lemon juice.
2. Use a large trifle dish and layer 1/3 of the banana pudding to the bottom.
3. Top with ⅓ of the sliced bananas.
4. Add a layer of Vanilla Wafers around the edges of the trifle.
5. Add ⅓ of the crunches and top of the sliced bananas and repeat the layers.
6. Pile or pipe the remaining whipped topping on the top.
7. Garnish with the remaining crunchies and sliced bananas.

TURTLE BANANA PUDDING

from the National Banana Pudding Competition

INGREDIENTS

- Salted pecans
- Vanilla Wafers
- 1 bag of mini turtle candies
- Salted Caramel ice cream topping
- Hot Fudge ice cream topping
- 6 Bananas

INSTRUCTIONS

1. Follow the instructions for Easy Banana Pudding Recipe on page 66.

SALTED CARAMEL WHIPPED CREAM

INGREDIENTS

- 1-1/2 cup heavy cream
- 3 tablespoons instant banana pudding
- 1/3 cup salted caramel, store-bought or homemade

INSTRUCTIONS

1. Whip the heavy cream and pudding mix until soft peaks form.
2. Add the salted caramel and continue whipping until stiff peaks form.

LAYER THE TURTLE BANANA PUDDING

1. Slice bananas and lightly drizzle them with lemon juice.
2. In a 9 x 13 baking dish, layer half the pudding and half the bananas.
3. Drizzle bananas with salted caramel and fudge sauce.
4. Add a layer of Vanilla Wafers.
5. Repeat the layers ending with Vanilla Wafers.
6. Pipe salted caramel whipped cream swirls using a 1M pastry tip and pastry bag. Pipe swirls around the edges of the pudding.
7. When ready to serve, top each whipped cream swirl with a Vanilla Wafer, slice of banana, and turtle candy.
8. Fill the center of the pudding with the salted pecans.

TOASTED SALTED PECANS

INGREDIENTS

- 2 cups pecans, chopped
- 4 tablespoons butter
- 1-1/2 teaspoon fine sea salt

INSTRUCTIONS

1. In a small skillet, melt the butter and add the pecans. Sprinkle with salt. Toast until lightly tan and it has a nutty aroma. Let the pecans completely cool.

INDIVIDUAL BANANA PUDDING CHEESECAKES

VANILLA WAFER CRUST

INGREDIENTS

- 1-1/2 cup crushed Vanilla Wafers
- 6 tablespoons butter, melted
- ¼ cup brown sugar
- 1 teaspoon cinnamon

INSTRUCTIONS

1. Preheat the oven to 325 degrees F.
2. Use a 12-cup mini cheesecake pan with removable bottoms or a 12-cup regular muffin tin. Use cupcake liners with the muffin tin. Spray pans with baking spray.
3. Place the Vanilla Wafers in a food processor and process until fine crumbs or crush the wafers in a ziplock bag using a mallet or rolling pin.
4. Combine the melted butter, sugar, and cinnamon with the crumbs.
5. Evenly distribute the crumb mixture between the bottom of each cupcake liner and press down using a tablespoon or small glass. (A spice jar works well.)
6. Bake the crust for 5 minutes.
7. Cool to room temperature.

CHEESECAKE

INGREDIENTS

- 16 ounces cream cheese, softened
- 3/4 cup sugar
- 2 teaspoons pure vanilla
- 1 teaspoon banana extract
- ¼ cup sour cream
- ¼ cup banana, mashed
- 2 large eggs

INSTRUCTIONS

1. Preheat oven 325.
2. Using an electric mixer, combine the cream cheese, sugar, vanilla, banana extract, and sour cream and beat until smooth.
3. Incorporate the mashed banana.
4. Add eggs one at a time and beat until incorporated. Do not overbeat the batter.
5. Use a regular size ice cream scoop and scoop even amounts of cheesecake filling on top of each graham cracker crust.
6. Bake cheesecakes for 20 to 25 minutes until the filling is almost set. The center will giggle slightly.
7. Remove from the oven and cool before placing in the refrigerator.
8. When serving, add a spoonful of banana pudding to each one.

BANANA PUDDING

INGREDIENTS

- 2 cups half-and-half
- ½ banana
- ¾ cup sugar
- 4 egg yolks
- ¼ cup cornstarch
- 1/8 teaspoon salt
- 1 teaspoon vanilla paste
- 1 teaspoon of banana extract
- 2 tablespoons butter
- ½ cup heavy cream, whipped

INSTRUCTIONS

1. Use a blender to combine the half-and-half and ½ banana until smooth.
2. Heat half-and-half, banana, and sugar in the microwave for about three to four minutes on full power. The half-and-half should be steaming but not boiling. Stir it well before and after heating. You can heat the milk on the stove, but it will burn and needs to be watched.
3. Whisk egg yolks until a pale-yellow color. Whisk in cornstarch and salt with the egg yolks. Once the egg yolks and cornstarch are light and smooth, it is ready for the milk.
4. Temper Eggs: Place a silicone mat or a towel under your bowl to prevent it from slipping. Slowly drizzle a cup of warm milk over the egg mixture while constantly whisking. Use one hand to drizzle the milk into the egg yolks and one hand to whisk the mixture. Whisk in the remaining warm milk.
5. Pour the mixture into a clean pot and whisk over medium-low heat until it thickens.
6. Cook while whisking until the pudding is thick, about 180 F. degrees.
7. Pull the pudding on and off the burner if needed to whisk. It should coat the back of a spoon. When you run your fingers through it, and the pudding doesn't meet, it's ready.
8. Remove from the heat, add the butter, banana extract, and vanilla, and whisk until the butter melts and incorporates.
9. Place in a bowl, and cover with plastic wrap directly on the pudding to prevent skin from forming.
10. Cool at room temperature.
11. Place in the refrigerator until firm for a couple of hours.
12. Whip the heavy cream to stiff peaks.
13. Fold the whipped cream into the pudding.
14. When serving, top each cheesecake with a tablespoon of pudding, a slice of banana, and a Vanilla Wafer.

BANANA PUDDING COOKIE CUPS

COOKIE CUPS

INGREDIENTS

- 1 cup butter, softened
- 1-1/2 cups sugar
- 2 eggs
- 3 teaspoons pure vanilla extract
- 2-3/4 cups of all-purpose flour
- 1 teaspoon baking powder
- 1 teaspoon salt
- 1/2 cup melted caramel chips

INSTRUCTIONS

1. Preheat oven to 350 degrees. Spray two regular-size muffin tins with cooking spray.
2. In a stand mixer, cream the butter and sugar until fluffy.
3. Add eggs one at a time and continue beating until incorporated.
4. Mix in the vanilla.
5. Whisk the flour, baking powder, and salt together.
6. Add the dry ingredients to the butter, sugar, and egg mixture just until combined.
7. Use a regular ice cream scoop (3 tablespoons), and scoop dough into muffin tins.
8. Bake for 12 minutes. The edges will be slightly golden.
9. Remove from the oven and use a tablespoon, small round lid, or container to press an indention in the middle of the cookie while they are hot. (A spice jar works well.)
10. Melt the caramel chips in the microwave for 30 seconds and stir until smooth.
11. Brush the inside of each cookie with melted caramel chips.
12. Cool for ten minutes in the pan.
13. Remove from the pan and place on a large baking sheet.
14. Cool completely.

TIP

The melted caramel acts as a barrier to keep the cookie cups from getting soggy. Best if eaten on the same day.

BANANA PUDDING

INGREDIENTS

- 4 cups half-and-half
- 1 banana
- 1-1/2 cups sugar
- 6 egg yolks
- 1/3 cup cornstarch
- 1/4 teaspoon salt
- 1 teaspoon of banana extract
- 2 teaspoons vanilla paste
- 4 tablespoons butter
- ½ cup whipping cream

INSTRUCTIONS

1. Use a blender to combine the half-and-half and banana until smooth.
2. Heat half-and-half, banana, and sugar in the microwave for about three to four minutes on full power. The half-and-half should be steaming but not boiling. Stir it well before and after heating. You can heat the milk on the stove, but it will burn and needs to be watched.
3. Whisk egg yolks until a pale-yellow color. Whisk in cornstarch and salt with the egg yolks. Once the egg yolks and cornstarch are light and smooth, it is ready for the milk.
4. Temper Eggs: Place a silicone mat or a towel under your bowl to prevent it from slipping. Slowly drizzle a cup of warm milk over the egg mixture while constantly whisking. Use one hand to drizzle the milk into the egg yolks and one hand to whisk the mixture. Whisk in the remaining warm milk.
5. Pour the mixture into a clean pot and whisk over medium-low heat until it thickens.
6. Cook while whisking until the pudding is thick, about 180 F. degrees.
7. Pull the pudding on and off the burner if needed to whisk. It should coat the back of a spoon. When you run your fingers through it, it should remain separated.
8. Remove from the heat, add the butter, banana extract, and vanilla, and whisk until the butter melts and incorporates.
9. Place in a bowl, and cover with plastic wrap directly on the pudding to prevent skin from forming.
10. Cool at room temperature and refrigerate.
11. When ready to serve, whip half a cup of heavy cream until stiff peaks and fold it into the pudding.
12. Top each cookie cup with pudding.
13. When serving, garnish with slices of banana and vanilla wafers.

EASY BANANA PUDDING POKE CAKE

Here is the most popular easy dessert recipe from my blog. Year after year my easy banana pudding poke cake had the most hits. It is made using a cake mix, instant pudding mix, and frozen whipped cream. You can't get any easier or more delicious. Add the banana slices when plating to keep them fresh.

INGREDIENTS

- 1 (15-ounce) box of yellow cake mix
- 2 (3.4 ounces) box instant pudding banana or vanilla flavor
- 3 cups milk
- 3 bananas, sliced and drizzled with lemon juice
- 8 ounces whipped topping thawed
- 8 ounces English toffee pieces

INSTRUCTIONS

1. Bake the cake using the package ingredients and instructions for a 9 x 13 bake.
2. Once the cake has cooled completely, poke holes about 1/2 inch apart all over the cake. Use the back of a wooden spoon.
3. Combine the pudding mix and milk.
4. Whisk until thoroughly combined and let set for a couple of minutes.
5. Pour over the cake.
6. Refrigerate the pudding cake until firm, 1-2 hours.
7. Spread the whipped topping on top.
8. Sprinkle with vanilla wafer crunchies and English toffee pieces.
9. When plating, add slices of banana on top of each serving.
10. Keep refrigerated.

VANILLA CRUNCHIES

INGREDIENTS

- 2 cups crushed Vanilla Wafer cookies
- ¾ cup pecans, finely chopped
- ¼ cup brown sugar
- 10 tablespoons butter, melted
- 1 teaspoon cinnamon

INSTRUCTIONS

1. Crush the Vanilla wafers in a ziplock bag or a food processor.
2. Transfer crumbs to a bowl and stir in pecans, sugar, butter, and cinnamon.
3. Spread out on a large baking sheet.
4. Bake at 350 degrees for 15 minutes. Cool completely and break into pieces.

TIP

You can replace the crunchies with Vanilla Wafers, but they get soggy faster.

MADE-FROM-SCRATCH BANANA PUDDING CAKE

Homemade yellow cake is a family favorite. I use this cake recipe to make two-layer birthday cakes often by adding chocolate buttercream and sprinkles. The yellow cake is also delicious with banana pudding in this made-from-scratch banana pudding cake. The earlier Banana Pudding Poke Cake recipe is elevated with this made-from-scratch cake, pudding, and whipped cream.

MADE-FROM-SCRATCH YELLOW CAKE

INGREDIENTS

- ½ cup softened butter
- ½ cup vegetable oil
- 1-¾ cup sugar
- 4 large eggs, room temperature
- 1 tablespoon pure vanilla extract
- 3 cups all-purpose flour, 390 grams
- 1 tablespoon baking powder
- ½ teaspoon salt
- 1-¼ cup buttermilk

INSTRUCTIONS

1. Preheat the oven to 350 degrees.
2. Prepare a 9 x 13 baking pan by spraying it with a baking spray and lined with parchment paper.
3. Whisk the flour, salt, and baking powder.
4. Cream the butter, oil, and sugar until creamy, 3 - 4 minutes using an electric mixer.
5. Add the eggs, one at a time. Combine well before adding the next egg.
6. Blend in the vanilla.
7. Add half of the dry ingredients into the mixer just until combined.
8. Add the buttermilk and mix just until combined.
9. Blend in the other half of the dry ingredients by hand. The batter may have some small lumps.
10. Pour the batter into the prepared baking pan.
11. Bake for 25 minutes or until a toothpick inserted in the center is mostly clean. The cake should spring back when touched. The internal temperature should be around 200 F. degrees.
12. Cool it before poking holes in it.

BANANA PUDDING

INGREDIENTS

- 2 cups half-and-half
- ½ banana
- 3/4 cup sugar
- 4 egg yolks
- 1/4 cup cornstarch
- 1/8 teaspoon salt
- 1 teaspoon pure vanilla extract
- 1 teaspoon of banana extract
- 2 tablespoons butter
- 2 medium bananas, sliced
- ½ cup salted pecans, chopped
- 3 bananas, sliced and drizzled with lemon juice
- Heath bar/English toffee pieces

INSTRUCTIONS

1. Use a blender to combine the half-and-half and ½ banana until smooth.
2. Heat half-and-half, banana, and sugar in the microwave for about three to four minutes on full power. The half-and-half should be steaming but not boiling. Stir it well before and after heating. You can heat the milk on the stove, but it will burn and needs to be watched.
3. Whisk egg yolks until a pale-yellow color. Whisk in cornstarch and salt with the egg yolks. Once the egg yolks and cornstarch are light and smooth, it is ready for the milk.
4. Temper Eggs: Place a silicone mat or a towel under your bowl to prevent it from slipping. Slowly drizzle a cup of warm milk over the egg mixture while constantly whisking. Use one hand to drizzle the milk into the egg yolks and one hand to whisk the mixture. Whisk in the remaining warm milk.
5. Pour the mixture into a clean pot and whisk over medium-low heat until it thickens.
6. Cook while whisking until the pudding is thick, about 175 F. - 180 F. degrees.
7. Pull the pudding on and off the burner if needed to whisk. It should coat the back of a spoon. When you run your fingers through it, it should remain separated.
8. Remove from the heat, add the butter, banana extract, and vanilla, and whisk until the butter melts and incorporates.
9. Place in a bowl, and cover with plastic wrap directly on the pudding to prevent skin from forming.
10. Cool at room temperature. The pudding will be thick.
11. Whip the heavy cream and fold a cup into the pudding.
12. Layer it on the cake.
13. Spread the remaining whipped cream over the pudding.
14. Top with the vanilla wafer crunchies and Heath bar/English toffee pieces.
15. When plating, add slices of banana to each serving.
16. Keep refrigerated.

WHIPPED CREAM

INGREDIENTS

- 1-1/2 cup heavy whipping cream
- 3/4 cup powdered sugar
- 1-1/2 teaspoons pure vanilla extract

INSTRUCTIONS

1. Beat whipped cream at medium speed using an electric mixer until foamy.
2. Slowly add the powdered sugar while continuing to beat.
3. Add the vanilla and beat until stiff peaks form.

VANILLA CRUNCHIES

INGREDIENTS

- 2 cups crushed Vanilla Wafer cookies
- 1 cup pecans, finely chopped
- ¼ cup brown sugar
- 11 tablespoons butter, melted
- 1 teaspoon cinnamon

INSTRUCTIONS

1. Crush the Vanilla wafers in a ziplock bag or a food processor.
2. Transfer crumbs to a bowl and stir in pecans, sugar, butter, and cinnamon.
3. Spread out on a large baking sheet.
4. Bake at 350 degrees for 15 minutes. Cool completely and break into pieces.

TIP

You can replace the crunchies with Vanilla Wafers, but they get soggy faster.

CREAMY BERRY DESSERTS

Taste and see that the Lord is good; blessed is the one who takes refuge in him. Psalm 34:8 NIV

Berries and Cream are the perfect treats. You'll find easy recipes in this chapter to whip up on a hot summer day or made-from-scratch recipes to impress your guests.

I use fresh orange juice and orange zest in several of the recipes. Citrus and berries go well together. My father was originally from Florida and told us stories about growing up in the Florida orange groves. After he passed, I purchased several potted orange and lemon trees to remind me of him. They produce lots of oranges which I use in my desserts.

I also use a lot of freeze-dried berries, which adds loads of flavor and color to desserts.

BLUEBERRY CREAM PIE

with Blueberry Whipped Cream

Crunchy Creamy Goodness is what I call this blueberry cream pie. The pecan shortbread crust is the perfect crunchy element.

PECAN SHORTBREAD CRUST

INGREDIENTS

- 1/2 cup butter, melted
- 1 cup all-purpose flour
- 1/2 cup pecans, chopped pieces
- 1/3 cup brown sugar
- ¼ teaspoon salt

INSTRUCTIONS

1. In a bowl, stir together the butter, flour, pecans, brown sugar, and salt until it comes together. The mixture should be crumbly. Don't overmix the dough.
2. Press the mixture into a lightly buttered 9-inch pie pan.
3. Bake 325 F. degrees for 15 minutes or until golden. Cool the crust completely.

CREAM CHEESE FILLING

INGREDIENTS

- 1 (8 ounces) of cream cheese
- 1 cup powdered sugar
- 1 cup heavy cream, whipped stiff
- 1 teaspoon vanilla
- Zest from one large orange

INSTRUCTIONS

1. Whip the heavy cream with a half cup of powdered sugar on medium speed until stiff peaks, 3 to 5 minutes. Transfer the cream to a bowl.
2. In the same mixer, (no need to clean it), beat the cream cheese and the remaining half cup of powdered sugar on medium speed until creamy.
3. Scrape down the bowl again. Mix in the vanilla and orange zest.
4. Using a rubber spatula, gently fold the whipped heavy cream into the cream cheese mixture.
5. Spread the cream cheese filling in the cooled pie crust and top with the blueberry filling.

BLUEBERRY PIE TOPPING

INGREDIENTS

- 1 tablespoon cornstarch
- 1 tablespoon water
- 1/4 cup granulated sugar
- 1/4 cup brown sugar
- ½ teaspoon cinnamon
- Zest from one large orange
- ¼ cup orange juice
- 3 cups blueberries, fresh or frozen, rinsed and stems removed

INSTRUCTIONS

1. In a small bowl, whisk together the cornstarch and water until dissolved.
2. Combine two cups of blueberries, sugar, brown sugar, orange juice, and zest in a pot. Stir until the sugars dissolve and the mixture begins to boil.
3. Once the berries start to boil, add the cornstarch mixture. Cook and stir until thick, about 4-5 minutes. Remove from heat.
4. Pour the mixture into a heat-proof bowl.
5. Gently stir in the remaining cup of blueberries.
6. Cover and refrigerate until completely cool.
7. When ready to serve, mound homemade whipped cream on top of it.
8. Serve with Blueberry Whipped Cream

TIP

Try a can of blueberry pie filling to top this cream cheese pie filling.

BLUEBERRY WHIPPED CREAM

INGREDIENTS

- 1-1/2 cups heavy cream
- 1-ounce package of freeze-dried blueberries (4 tablespoons powder)
- 1/2 cup confectioners' sugar

INSTRUCTIONS

1. Add the freeze-dried berries to a food processor. Pulse into powder.
2. Whip the heavy cream, blueberry powder, and powdered sugar until stiff peaks form using an electric mixer. The extra powdered sugar helps stabilize the whipped cream.
3. Use a pastry bag fitted with a #1M tip.
4. Hold the bag vertically above the pie on the outer edge. Place the tip slightly above the pie and apply pressure. As you pipe, slowly lift the bag and make two small swirls on top of each other before releasing pressure and pulling up. Do this around the pie.

ELEGANT STRAWBERRY PIE
with Whipped Cream

This strawberry tart is not only creamy and delicious but stunning. The freeze-dried fruit brings out more of the strawberry flavor. The strawberries are arranged in an elegant flower.

GRAHAM CRACKER CRUST

INGREDIENTS

- 1-1/2 cups graham cracker crumbs
- 6 tablespoons butter, melted
- 1/4 cup brown sugar
- 1-1/2 teaspoon cinnamon

INSTRUCTIONS

1. Place the graham crackers in a food processor and process until fine crumbs. You can also break the sheets up and place them in a ziplock bag. Use a mallet or rolling pin to crush the crackers into crumbs.
2. Combine the melted butter, sugar, and cinnamon with your crumbs.
3. Press over the bottom and sides of a 9-inch pie or tart pan.
4. Bake at 350 degrees for 10 minutes.

STRAWBERRY FILLING

INGREDIENTS

- 2 (8 oz) packages of full-fat cream cheese, softened
- 1 cup powdered sugar
- 1 package (1 oz) of freeze-dried strawberries
- 1 tablespoon fresh lemon juice
- 1 teaspoon vanilla
- 8-oz frozen whipping topping, thawed

INSTRUCTIONS

1. Use a food processor to pulse the freeze-dried strawberries into powder.
2. In a large bowl, combine the cream cheese, sugar, freeze-dried strawberries, lemon juice, and vanilla until creamy.
3. Fold two cups of whipped topping into the cream cheese mixture.
4. Spread into the pie crust and level it.
5. Spread the remaining whipped topping over the strawberry filling.

STRAWBERRY DESIGN

INGREDIENTS

- 1-pint strawberries
- Strawberry jelly
- Lemon, zested

INSTRUCTIONS

1. Wash and slice the strawberries lengthwise in thin slices. An egg slicer will slice the strawberries perfectly.
2. Starting on the outside edges, arrange strawberries with the points sticking out in a circle around the pie until it is covered.
3. Microwave two tablespoons of jelly for 15 to 20 seconds until melted.
4. Brush over strawberries to add shine. Repeat the glaze just before serving.
5. Zest the lemon over the strawberries.
6. Serve with strawberry whipped cream.

TIP

Use a 1M pastry tip and pipe stars around the edge of the pie. You can also start your strawberry slices at the edge of the pie.

EASY BLUEBERRY COBBLER
with Oatmeal Butterscotch Cookie Crumble

The combination of butterscotch, oatmeal, and berries is fabulous. Elevate this simple dessert with creme anglaise or ice cream. It is a deliciously warm and gooey treat to eat in the winter using frozen berries or perfect for the summer using fresh berries.

COBBLER

INGREDIENTS

- 6 cups berries, fresh or frozen but not thawed
- 1/2 cups sugar
- ⅓ cup brown sugar
- ⅓ cup flour
- 1 teaspoon cinnamon

INSTRUCTIONS

1. Preheat oven to 350 degrees.
2. Spray a 9 x 13 baking dish.
3. Toss the blueberries with sugar, brown sugar, flour, and cinnamon and set aside, stirring a few times.

OATMEAL BUTTERSCOTCH COOKIE CRUMBLE

INGREDIENTS

- 3/4 cup all-purpose flour
- 3/4 cup rolled oats
- 3/4 cup brown sugar
- 1/3 cup pecans, finely chopped
- 1 teaspoon cinnamon
- 1/2 teaspoon salt
- ½ cup butter, melted
- 1 cup butterscotch chips

INSTRUCTIONS

1. Whisk the flour, oats, brown sugar, pecans, cinnamon, and salt.
2. Add the melted butter and stir using a rubber spatula.
3. Stir in a cup of butterscotch chips.
4. The mixture should come together and be crumbly.

ADDITIONAL INGREDIENTS

- 2 tablespoons butter, melted in the skillet
- 1 cup butterscotch chips

INSTRUCTIONS

1. Preheat oven to 350 degrees.
2. Melt the butter in a 10-inch skillet or a 9 x 13 baking dish and swirl around the edges.
3. Add the berries to the buttered skillet.
4. Add the cup of butterscotch chips on top of the berries.
5. Sprinkle the cookie crumble on top on top of the chips.
6. Bake for 45 minutes or until golden brown.
7. The cobbler should be bubbling around the edges.
8. Serve with vanilla ice cream

BLACKBERRY ORANGE CREAM TART

I have two blackberry bushes that give me an abundance of blackberries each summer. This treat is a quick and easy way to use them.

CRUST

INGREDIENTS

- 1-3/4 cups graham cracker crumbs
- 7 tablespoons butter, melted
- 1/4 cup brown sugar
- 1-1/2 teaspoon pumpkin pie spice
- Zest from one orange

INSTRUCTIONS

1. Place the graham crackers in a food processor and process until fine crumbs. You can also break up the sheets and place them in a ziplock bag. Use a mallet or rolling pin to crush the crackers into crumbs.
2. Combine the melted butter, brown sugar, pumpkin pie spice, and orange zest with the crumbs.
3. Press over the bottom and sides of a 10" tart pan or 9x13 dish.
4. Bake at 350 degrees for 10 - 12 minutes.

FILLING

INGREDIENTS

- 2 - (8-ounces) packages of cream cheese softened
- 3/4 cup sugar
- 2 tablespoons fresh orange zest
- 8 ounces frozen whipped topping, thawed
- 4 cups fresh blackberries, depending on the size of the berries
- 1/2 cup orange marmalade
- 1 large orange, zested

INSTRUCTIONS

1. Using an electric mixer on medium speed, beat the cream cheese, sugar, and orange zest until creamy.
2. Fold in the whipped topping.
3. Pour into the prepared tart crust.
4. Refrigerate for a couple of hours before adding the berries
5. Remove from the refrigerator and arrange the fresh blackberries in circles on the crust.
6. Before serving, melt the orange marmalade in the microwave for 30 - 45 seconds.
7. Brush over blackberries.
8. Zest another orange over the top of the tart for extra flavor and a beautiful presentation.

BERRY TRIFLE

with Fresh Berries and Homemade Pound Cake

This berry trifle is an eye-catcher and the perfect centerpiece for a summer party. Use the flavorful homemade pound cake recipe below or, for a quicker version, purchase a store-bought pound cake. However you prepare it, you can't beat this summer treat.

TIP

Half the ingredients and layer in individual glasses for a smaller gathering.

TRIFLE

INGREDIENTS

- 1 pint of fresh strawberries, sliced
- 1 pint of fresh blueberries
- 1 pint of fresh blackberries
- 1 large lemon, zested and juiced
- ⅓ cup sugar

INSTRUCTIONS

1. Wash berries and slice strawberries in thirds. Toss the berries with sugar, lemon zest, and juice. Let the berries set for thirty minutes to begin releasing their juices.

CREAM

INGREDIENTS

- 2 cups heavy cream, whipped
- 2 (8 oz) cream cheese
- 1 cup sugar
- 1 cup lemon curd, completely cooled
- ½ Pound cake, cut into one-inch pieces (See below or use store-bought cake for a short-cut)

INSTRUCTIONS

1. Using an electric mixer, beat the heavy cream with ½ cup of the sugar until stiff peaks.
2. In a separate bowl, whip the cream cheese with the remaining ½ cup of sugar until smooth.
3. Add the lemon curd to the cream cheese and mix until incorporated.
4. Fold in two cups of whipped cream.
5. Spoon a layer of lemon cream into a large trifle bowl.
6. Add a layer of the pound cake pieces.
7. Top the pound cake with the berries.
8. Build three layers ending with berries on top.
9. Spread or pipe the remaining whipped cream on top.
10. Refrigerate until ready to serve.
11. Best if eaten on the same day.
12. Garnish with additional berries and lemon slices.

MOIST FLAVORFUL LEMON POUND CAKE

When my special needs son, Caleb, was around two, I sat him on the kitchen counter and baked this cake weekly. When we finished, we'd take it to the neighbors. Caleb has Cerebral Palsy and seizures. Baking was a great activity to help him with his memory and fine motor skills. He loved it and still does today.

This cake is known by family and friends as Caleb's Comfort Cake. You can read about Caleb's story in my memoir, Heartaches to Blessings.

This pound cake is fabulous by itself and can be elevated with all of the sauces in this cookbook, plus it is fantastic in this trifle.

INGREDIENTS

- 1 cup butter, softened
- 1/2 cup butter-flavored shortening
- 3 cups of sugar
- 5 eggs
- 3/4 cup of sour cream
- 2 teaspoons lemon extract
- 1 tablespoon pure vanilla extract
- Zest two large lemons
- 1 teaspoon salt
- 1 teaspoon baking powder
- 3 cups all-purpose flour, 390 grams
- 3/4 cup buttermilk

INSTRUCTIONS

1. Preheat oven to 325 degrees.
2. With an electric mixer, cream butter and shortening until light and fluffy.
3. Drizzle the sugar in the mixture, and continue beating until light and creamy, four to five minutes.
4. Add five eggs one at a time. When the yolks disappear add another egg.
5. Blend in the sour cream.
6. Mix in lemon extract, pure vanilla, and lemon zest.
7. Sift or whisk the flour, baking powder, and salt.
8. Turn the mixer to low and add half the flour mixture.
9. Add the buttermilk.
10. Add the rest of the dry ingredients.
11. Bake at 325 degrees for 1 hour and 15 minutes. The internal temperature should be around 205 F. to 210 F. degrees.
12. Remove from the oven and cool for about fifteen minutes.
13. Flip it over on a cooling rack to cool completely.

FRESH BERRY DESSERT PIZZA
with Cookie Crust

When my kids were growing up, this was one of their favorite treats. It's a hit at any kid's party. It's worth the effort to whip up this fruity pizza, but if you're in a hurry, a store-bought sugar cookie dough roll works well.

COOKIE CRUST

INGREDIENTS

- 1 cup butter, softened
- 1-1/2 cup sugar
- 1 egg
- 2 teaspoons pure vanilla extract
- 2-3/4 cups of all-purpose flour
- 1 teaspoon baking powder
- 1/2 teaspoon salt

INSTRUCTIONS

1. Cream the butter and sugar together until smooth.
2. Add the egg and vanilla.
3. Scrape down the side of the mixer and continue combining.
4. Whisk the dry ingredients together and add to the mixer.
5. Once combined, cover the plastic wrap and rest it in the refrigerator for thirty minutes.
6. Preheat oven to 350 degrees.
7. Grease a 12-inch rimmed pizza pan with baking spray.
8. Remove the dough from the refrigerator and press on the pizza pan.
9. Bake for 16 to 18 minutes until lightly browned.
10. Cool completely before adding the cream cheese mixture.

CREAM

INGREDIENTS

- 1 (8 oz) cream cheese, softened
- 7 ounces marshmallow cream
- 1 large orange, zested
- 1 teaspoon pure vanilla

INSTRUCTIONS

1. Whip the cream cheese and marshmallow cream until smooth and creamy.
2. Add the orange zest and vanilla.
3. Spread the topping over the cooled cookie and refrigerate until firm.

BERRIES

INGREDIENTS

- 4 cups fresh berries including strawberries, rinsed, stems removed, washed, and dried
- 1/2 cup orange marmalade
- 1 large orange, zested

INSTRUCTIONS

1. Slice the strawberries with the ends pointing up.
2. Arrange the strawberries on the outside of the cookie with the point of the strawberry facing out.
3. Continue making circles of fruit working your way to the center.
4. Melt the marmalade for 30 seconds in the microwave and mix well. It may need a few more seconds.
5. Just before serving, brush the berries with melted orange marmalade and the orange zest.

CHEESECAKE

Topped with Fresh Berries, Berry Compote, and White Chocolate Sauce

Cheesecake and berries go together like peanut butter and jelly. They are made for each other. It is elevated with a berry compote and white chocolate sauce. The tart berries with the sweet white chocolate are a mouth-watering combination.

Cheesecakes include simple ingredients. It's the method that matters when the goal is to achieve a silky dessert. You can achieve the perfect cheesecake with these tips including checking the internal temperature of the cheesecake.

CRUST

INGREDIENTS

- 2 cups graham cracker crumbs
- 9 tablespoons butter, melted
- 1/3 cup brown sugar
- 1-1/2 teaspoon cinnamon

INSTRUCTIONS

1. Preheat the oven to 325 F. degrees.
2. Combine graham cracker crumbs, melted butter, brown sugar, and cinnamon.
3. Press firmly over the bottom of a 9-inch or 10-inch springform pan with sides at least 3" inches tall.
4. Bake for 10 minutes.

CHEESECAKE FILLING

INGREDIENTS

- 4 (8-oz.) full-fat cream cheese, softened
- 1-1/2 cup sugar
- 2 tablespoons cornstarch
- 1 tablespoon pure vanilla paste
- 4 large eggs
- 1/2 cup sour cream
- ¼ cup heavy cream

INSTRUCTIONS

1. Preheat oven to 325 degrees.
2. Boil a kettle of water.
3. Using an electric mixer, whip the cream cheese until smooth.
4. Slowly drizzle in the sugar and mix until combined.
5. Add the cornstarch and vanilla.
6. Mix in the eggs one at a time until combined.
7. Stir in the sour cream and heavy cream and mix until combined. Don't over-mix.
8. Tap the mixing bowl on the counter several times to release air bubbles.
9. Spread the cheesecake batter in the 9" springform pan.
10. Set the cheesecake pan in a slow cooker bag and twist together the sides to make it fit snugly and tuck it in or tie it off.
11. Wrap a large piece of heavy-duty foil around the slow cooker bag up to the height of the pan and press it firmly to fit the pan.
12. Put the cheesecake in the oven on a roasting pan.
13. Carefully pour the hot water around the cheesecake.
14. Bake cheesecakes for 70-75 minutes or until the filling is almost set. Check the temperature after an hour.
15. Insert a thermometer into the center of the cheesecake. It should read 150 degrees.
16. Leave your cheesecake in the oven and pull the rack out.
17. Run a knife or small offset spatula around the edge of the cake pan, preventing the cheesecake from sticking to the sides. As the cake cools, it will contract and pull away from the sides of the pan. If the cheesecake sticks to the edges, it will crack.
18. Crack the oven and let the cheesecake remain in it for thirty minutes. Leaving the cheesecake in the oven with the oven off and the door cracked, helps prevent cracks but leaving it too long will dry it out.
19. After a cheesecake is in the refrigerator all night, remove the side walls. Once removed from the pan, flip it over on a cake board. Run a sharp knife between the cheesecake and the bottom of the springform pan. Now, remove the pan and parchment paper. Flip the cheesecake back over on a plate or another cake board.
20. Slice a cold cheesecake with a warmed chef's knife. Wipe the knife after each cut.
21. Top with fresh berries, berry compote, and white chocolate sauce.

BERRY COMPOTE

INGREDIENTS

- 4 cups mixed berries
- 3/4 cup sugar
- ¼ cup fresh orange juice
- Zest from large orange

INSTRUCTIONS

1. Add all ingredients to a medium size pot.
2. Cook until berries break down and juices are released, 10 to 15 minutes.
3. Strain through a fine mesh strainer to remove skin and seeds. If you don't mind the skin and seeds, skip this step. You could also use your food processor or an immersion blender to get rid of the skin and seeds.

WHITE CHOCOLATE SAUCE

INGREDIENTS

- 1 cup of white chocolate
- 1/3 cup heavy cream

INSTRUCTIONS

1. Heat the cream just until it starts to steam. Do not boil it. Pour it over the chocolate and let it set for two minutes. Whisk until creamy.

TIP

Warm the cream in the microwave.

INDIVIDUAL STRAWBERRY CHEESECAKES
with Lemon Whipped Cream

GOLDEN SANDWICH COOKIE CRUST

INGREDIENTS

- 12 Golden Stuffed Sandwich Cookies or Lemon Cookies

INSTRUCTIONS

1. Preheat the oven to 325 degrees F.
2. Use a mini cheesecake pan with removable bottoms or a 12-cup regular muffin tin. Use cupcake liners with the muffin tin. Spray pans with baking spray.
3. Place a cookie in each individual cheesecake or cupcake liner.

STRAWBERRY CHEESECAKE

INGREDIENTS

- 1 package (1 oz) of freeze-dried strawberries, crushed into powder
- 2 (8-oz packages) full-fat cream cheese, softened
- ¾ cup sugar
- ¼ cup sour cream
- 2 tablespoons heavy cream
- 1 teaspoon pure vanilla extract
- 2 eggs

INSTRUCTIONS

1. Preheat oven 325.
2. Pulse the freeze-dried strawberries into powder using a food processor.
3. Using an electric mixer, cream the strawberry powder, cream cheese, sugar, sour cream, heavy cream, and pure vanilla, and beat until smooth.
4. Add eggs one at a time and beat until incorporated. Do not overbeat the batter.
5. Use a regular size ice cream scoop and scoop even amounts of cheesecake filling on top of each graham cracker crust.
6. Bake cheesecakes for 20 to 25 minutes until the filling is almost set. The center will giggle slightly.
7. Let the cheesecakes cool before placing them in the refrigerator for at least two hours.
8. Pipe a dollop of lemon whipped cream on each cheesecake.

LEMON WHIPPED CREAM

INGREDIENTS

- 1 cup whipping cream
- 1/2 cup powdered sugar
- 1 tablespoon fresh lemon juice
- Zest from one lemon

INSTRUCTIONS

1. Beat heavy cream until it begins to thicken.
2. Gradually add sugar.
3. Continue beating and add lemon juice.
4. Beat until soft peaks form.
5. Fold lemon zest in by hand.

TIP

Not a lemon fan. Try topping these strawberry cheesecakes with chocolate ganache. Top with a chocolate-covered strawberry.

GANACHE

INGREDIENTS

- 1 cup semisweet chocolate chips
- ¼ cup heavy cream

INSTRUCTIONS

1. Heat the chocolate and cream in the microwave for one minute.
2. Remove from the microwave and stir until creamy.
3. Cool to room temperature.
4. Add a tablespoon to each cheesecake.

CREAMY CHOCOLATE DESSERTS

Chocolate Speak Volumes

This collection of my favorite chocolate desserts will fulfill your chocolate cravings but watch out, you'll be craving them. If you're looking for a quick and easy chocolate dessert or a chocolate dessert you can make from scratch to impress your guests, you'll find both here. Each recipe includes creamy flavors and textures that make your taste buds happy. It is the best way to say, "I love you".

CHOCOLATE CREAM PIE
with Whipped Cream Rosettes

Homemade chocolate pudding is delicious in this chocolate pie. To elevate it, I add a pecan shortbread crust for texture and a cream cheese filling for a little tang.

PECAN SHORTBREAD CRUST

INGREDIENTS

- 1/2 cup butter, melted
- 1 cup all-purpose flour
- 1/2 cup pecans, chopped pieces
- 1/3 cup brown sugar
- ¼ teaspoon salt

INSTRUCTIONS

1. In a bowl, stir together the butter, flour, pecans, brown sugar, and salt until it comes together. The mixture should be crumbly. Don't overmix the dough.
2. Press the mixture into a lightly buttered 9-inch pie pan.
3. Bake 325 F. degrees for 15 minutes or until golden. Cool the crust completely.

CREAM CHEESE LAYER

INGREDIENTS

- 1 cup heavy cream
- 1 cup powdered sugar
- 8 ounces of full-fat cream cheese softened
- 1 teaspoon pure vanilla

INSTRUCTIONS

1. Whip the heavy cream and powdered sugar until stiff peaks form.
2. Whip the cream cheese and vanilla until creamy.
3. Gently fold whipped cream into the cream cheese mixture.
4. Smooth out the creamy mixture in the pie crust.
5. Refrigerate

CHOCOLATE PUDDING

INGREDIENTS

- 2 cups half-and-half
- 1 cup sugar
- 4 egg yolks
- 1/4 cup cornstarch
- 1/4 teaspoon salt
- 2 tablespoons milk or half-and-half
- 1/3 cup cocoa
- 2 teaspoons pure vanilla extract
- 2 tablespoons butter

INSTRUCTIONS

1. Heat the half-and-half and sugar in the microwave for about four minutes until steaming but not boiling. You can also heat the milk on the stove but stir often. It will burn. Be extremely careful not to boil it.
2. In a medium bowl, whisk egg yolks until a pale-yellow color.
3. Whisk in cornstarch, salt, and 2 tablespoons milk, until light and smooth.
4. Whisk the cocoa powder into the egg and cornstarch mixture.
5. Temper Eggs: Place a silicone mat or a towel under your bowl to prevent it from slipping. Slowly drizzle the one cup of warm milk over the egg mixture while constantly whisking. Use one hand to drizzle the milk into the egg yolks and one hand to whisk the mixture. Once the bottom of the bowl is warm, slowly whisk in the remaining warm milk.
6. Pour the mixture into a clean pot and whisk over medium-low heat until it thickens.
7. Cook while constantly whisking until the pudding is glossy and thick. The custard should not come together when you run your finger across the back of a spoon covered in custard. It should be 175 F. 180 F. degrees.
8. Remove from the heat and whisk the butter and vanilla until the butter melts and is incorporated.
9. Place in a bowl and cover with plastic wrap directly on the filling to prevent skin from forming.
10. Cool at room temperature and refrigerate for thirty minutes until thick.
11. Whip the heavy cream and fold one cup into the pudding.
12. Spread over the cream cheese mixture and refrigerate.

WHIPPED TOPPING

INGREDIENTS

- 2 cups heavy whipping cream
- 1 cup powdered sugar, the extra sugar will stabilize the whipped cream to pipe the roses.
- 2 teaspoons pure vanilla extract
- Grated chocolate or chocolate curls

INSTRUCTIONS

1. Whip the heavy cream until soft peaks.
2. Gradually add the powdered sugar and vanilla. Beat until stiff peaks form.
3. Spread or pipe the remaining whipped cream on the chocolate cream pie.
4. Top with shaved chocolate.

WHIPPED CREAM ROSETTES

INSTRUCTIONS

1. Use a pastry bag fitted with a #1M tip.
2. Position the tip where you want the center of the rosette. With even pressure, squeeze the bag while moving clockwise in a circle. Stop squeezing just before you complete the circle. Continue building and stacking the rosettes.

MADE FROM SCRATCH CHOCOLATE LAYERED DESSERT

This dessert is elevated by making it from scratch. The homemade brownie, the cream cheese layer, homemade chocolate pudding, and homemade whipped cream are the perfect combination. It's what dreams are made of.

FIRST LAYER - HOMEMADE BROWNIES

INGREDIENTS

- 1 cup all-purpose flour
- 1/3 cup unsweetened dark cocoa powder sifted
- 1/2 teaspoon baking powder
- 1/2 teaspoon salt
- 2 cups granulated sugar
- 1 cup unsalted butter, melted and cooled to room temperature
- 2 teaspoons pure vanilla extract
- 4 eggs
- 2 cups semisweet chocolate chips

INSTRUCTIONS

1. Preheat the oven to 325 F. degrees.
2. Grease a 9 x 13 baking dish with cooking spray.
3. Cut a piece of parchment paper to fit on the bottom and sides of the pan. When the brownies cool, you can use the parchment paper to lift brownies from the pan. Spray with cooking spray.
4. Whisk the flour, cocoa powder, baking powder, and salt in a small bowl.
5. In a large bowl, mix the sugar, melted butter, and vanilla.
6. Slowly add the eggs one at a time to the sugar and butter mixture, fully incorporating each egg before adding the next.
7. Turn the mixer to low and add the flour mixture until combined.
8. Fold the chocolate chips into the batter with a large rubber spatula.
9. Pour the batter into the prepared dish and spread evenly.
10. Bake for 25 - 30 minutes until a cake tester or toothpick inserted into the center comes out with moist crumbs attached. Don't overcook the brownies.
11. Bake between 165 F. to 180 F. degrees. 165 F. degrees if you like fudgy brownies.
12. Let the brownies cool completely before adding the cream cheese layer.

SECOND LAYER – CREAM CHEESE LAYER

INGREDIENTS

- 2 (8-ounces) cream cheese
- 1-1/4 cup confectioners' sugar
- 1 cup heavy cream

INSTRUCTIONS

1. Whip the heavy cream and ½ cup of powdered sugar until stiff peaks form.
2. Combine the cream cheese and remaining powdered sugar until smooth and creamy.
3. Fold the whipped topping into the cream cheese mixture.
4. Layer the cream cheese mixture over the cooled brownies and refrigerate.

THIRD LAYER – HOMEMADE CHOCOLATE PUDDING

INGREDIENTS

- 2 cups half-and-half
- 1 cup sugar
- 4 egg yolks
- 1/4 cup cornstarch
- 1/4 teaspoon salt
- 2 tablespoons milk or half-and-half
- 1/3 cup cocoa
- 2 teaspoons pure vanilla extract
- 2 tablespoons butter
- ½ cup heavy cream

INSTRUCTIONS

1. Heat 2 cups half-and-half and sugar in the microwave for about four minutes until steaming but not boiling. You can also heat the milk on the stove but stir often, it will burn. Be extremely careful not to boil it.
2. In a medium bowl, whisk egg yolks until a pale-yellow color. Whisk in cornstarch, salt, and milk, until light and smooth.
3. Whisk the cocoa powder into the egg and cornstarch mixture.
4. Temper Eggs: Place a silicone mat or a towel under your bowl to prevent it from slipping. Slowly drizzle the one cup of warm milk over the egg mixture while constantly whisking. Use one hand to drizzle the milk into the egg yolks and one hand to whisk the mixture. Once the bottom of the bowl is warm, slowly whisk in the remaining warm milk.
5. Pour the mixture into a clean pot and whisk over medium-low heat until it thickens.
6. Cook while constantly whisking until the pudding is glossy and thick. The custard should not come together when you run your finger across the back of a spoon with custard on it. It should be 175 F. 180 F. degrees.
7. Remove from the heat and whisk the butter and vanilla until the butter melts and is incorporated.
8. Place in a bowl and cover with plastic wrap directly on the filling to prevent skin from forming.
9. Cool at room temperature and place in the refrigerator until firm.
10. Once the pudding is firm, whip the ½ cup heavy cream until stiff peaks form.
11. Fold whipped cream into the pudding.
12. Pour the chocolate mixture over the cream cheese mixture and spread it out.
13. Refrigerate until firm.

TIP
Top with chocolate curls.

FOURTH LAYER – WHIPPED CREAM

INGREDIENTS

- 2 cups heavy whipping cream
- 1 cup powdered sugar
- 1 teaspoon pure vanilla extract

INSTRUCTIONS

1. Combine ingredients and whip until stiff peaks.
2. Fold one cup of the whipped cream into the chocolate custard before spreading it over the cream cheese mixture.
3. Spread or pipe the remaining whipped cream over the chocolate custard.
4. The dollop swirls were made using a 1M piping tip.
5. Grate chocolate shavings over the whipped cream.

FOR AN ELEGANT PRESENTATION

Cut the brownies into bite-size pieces and layer them into an elegant glass or trifle dish. Layer brownies, chocolate candies, cream cheese mixer, pudding, and whipped cream, and repeat.

CHOCOLATE CHESS PIE
with Whipped Cream Rosettes

I can't get enough of this creamy Chocolate Chess Pie. It's that delicious! To elevate it, I pipe elegant whipped cream rosettes worthy of any special occasion. If the whipped cream roses look difficult, mound your whipped cream on the top of the pie or serve it on the plate.

FILLING

INGREDIENTS

- 2 cups sugar
- 1 tablespoon all-purpose flour
- 2 tablespoons yellow cornmeal
- 1/4 teaspoon salt
- 1/4 cup cocoa powder
- 4 egg yolks, beaten
- 1/2 cup butter, melted
- 1/2 cup buttermilk
- 2 teaspoons vanilla
- 1 pie crust, baked for 10 minutes
- ¾ cup chopped pecans, salted

INSTRUCTIONS

1. Preheat oven to 350 F degrees.
2. Using an electric mixer, beat eggs well.
3. Mix in sugar, flour, cornmeal, salt, and cocoa powder.
4. Add the melted butter, buttermilk, and vanilla.
5. Add this liquid mixture to the dry ingredients in the mixer and blend well.
6. Add a layer of salted pecans to the bottom of an unbaked pie shell.
7. Pour pie filling into the unbaked pie shell.
8. Bake at 350 F. degrees for 50 minutes or until the filling sets in the center. If necessary, cover the pie with aluminum foil for the last few minutes to prevent excessive browning.
9. Insert a toothpick in the center of the pie. It should be moist but not liquid. The pie will slightly giggle in the middle.
10. The internal temperature should be 185 F.-190 F. degrees.
11. Cool Completely.
12. Decorate with whipped cream roses.

WHIPPED CREAM ROSETTES

INGREDIENTS

- 1-1/2 cups heavy whipped cream, cold
- 3/4 cup confectioners' sugar
- 2 teaspoons pure vanilla extract

INSTRUCTIONS

1. Beat whipped cream using an electric mixer until foamy. Gradually, add the powdered sugar and vanilla while beating until stiff peaks form. The extra powdered sugar helps stabilize the whipped cream.
2. Use a pastry bag fitted with a #1M tip.
3. Position the pastry tip where you want the center of the rosette. With even pressure, squeeze the bag while moving clockwise in a circle. Stop squeezing just before you complete the circle.

CHOCOLATE SHAVINGS

WITHOUT THE WHIPPED CREAM.

BEST FUDGE PIE
with Large Whipped Cream Rose

This Fudge Pie is not a chocolate pie, and it's not a brownie pie. It's the best gooey chocolatey, fudgy pie with pecans. To elevate it for a beautiful presentation, I pipe a large whipped cream rose that covers the top of the pie.

FILLING

INGREDIENTS

- 1/2 cup butter
- 6 – 1-ounce squares of unsweetened chocolate
- 4 eggs lightly beaten
- 1-1/2 cups sugar
- 3 tablespoons light corn syrup
- 1/4 teaspoon salt
- 2 teaspoons pure vanilla extract
- 1/2 teaspoon butter flavor extract
- 1 cup chopped pecans
- 1 - 9- inch pie shell

INSTRUCTIONS

1. Melt the butter and chocolate in a double boiler or slowly in a pot over low heat.
2. Remove from heat once the chocolate melts. Stir it often. Chocolate will burn and will stick quickly.
3. Allow the chocolate to cool for five minutes.
4. Whisk the eggs, sugar, corn syrup, salt, vanilla, and butter extract.
5. Whisk in the melted chocolate to the egg mixture.
6. Continually whisk so you don't scramble the eggs.
7. Stir in the pecans.
8. Pour the chocolate mixture into the pie crust.
9. Bake 350 degrees for 45 minutes or until the center is set. It'll be soft to the touch. A toothpick inserted in the center will have wet crumbs.
10. The internal temperature should be 165 F. degrees.

WHIPPED CREAM FOR THE ROSE

INGREDIENTS

- 2 cups heavy whipping cream
- 1 cup powdered sugar
- 1 teaspoon vanilla paste

INSTRUCTIONS

1. Combine ingredients and whip until stiff peaks.
2. Use a pastry bag fitted with a large rose piping tip.
3. Position the tip where you want the center of the rosette. Add a dollop of whipped cream in the center of the pie. With even pressure, squeeze the bag while moving it in a circle. Add an odd number of pedals per row. Completely covering the pie in a large rosette.

SERVED WITH ICE CREAM

CHEESECAKE

Covered in Rich Brownie Pieces and Chocolate Fudge

Talk about a big eye-catching dessert! This cheesecake covered with gooey brownies and chocolate fudge is delicious and a head-turning centerpiece. It takes a couple of days to prepare. The cheesecake needs to be refrigerated overnight before stacking the brownies on it.

As I mentioned earlier, cheesecakes include simple ingredients. It's the method that matters when baking a cheesecake to achieve a silky dessert. You can achieve the perfect cheesecake with these tips including checking the internal temperature of the cheesecake.

CHOCOLATE GRAHAM CRACKER CRUST

INGREDIENTS

- 2 cups graham cracker crumbs
- 1/3 cup brown sugar
- 1/2 cup cocoa powder
- 3/4 cup butter, melted

INSTRUCTIONS

1. Melt the butter in the microwave.
2. Stir in the cocoa powder.
3. Process the graham crackers in the food processor to make fine crumbs. You can also use a ziplock bag.
4. Transfer to the bowl with the cocoa powder and stir in the sugar.
5. Use the bottom of a glass and press the crumbs into a 9" or 10" springform pan.
6. Bake 325 F degrees for 10 minutes.

CHEESECAKE FILLING

INGREDIENTS

- 4 (8-oz.) full-fat cream cheese, softened
- 1-1/2 cup sugar
- 2 tablespoons cornstarch
- 1 tablespoon pure vanilla extract
- 4 large eggs
- 1/2 cup sour cream
- ¼ cup heavy cream

INSTRUCTIONS

1. Preheat oven to 325 degrees.
2. Boil a kettle of water.
3. Using an electric mixer, whip the cream cheese until smooth.
4. Slowly drizzle in the sugar and mix until combined.
5. Add the cornstarch and vanilla.
6. Mix in the eggs one at a time until just combined.
7. Stir in the sour cream and heavy cream and mix until combined. Don't overmix.
8. Tap the mixing bowl on the counter several times to release air bubbles.
9. This will depend on the size of your roasting pan.
10. Spread the cheesecake batter in the 9" springform pan.
11. Set the cheesecake pan in a slow cooker bag and twist together the sides to make it fit snugly and tuck it in or tie it off.
12. Wrap a large piece of heavy-duty foil around the slow cooker bag up to the height of the pan and press it firmly to fit the pan.
13. Put the cheesecake in the oven on a roasting pan.
14. Carefully pour the water around the cheesecake.
15. Bake cheesecakes for 70-75 minutes or until the filling is almost set.
16. Insert a thermometer into the center of the cheesecake. It should read 150 degrees when ready for the next steps.
17. Pull the oven rack out slightly and run a knife or small offset spatula around the edge of the cake pan, preventing the cheesecake from sticking to the sides. As the cake cools, it will contract and pull away from the sides of the pan. If the cheesecake sticks to the edges, it will crack.
18. Crack the oven and let the cheesecake remain in it for thirty minutes. Leaving the cheesecake in the oven with the oven off and the door cracked, helps prevent cracks but leaving it too long will dry it out.
19. After a cheesecake is in the refrigerator all night, remove the side walls. Once removed from the pan, flip it over on a cake board. Run a sharp knife between the cheesecake and the bottom of the springform pan. Now, remove the pan and parchment paper. Flip the cheesecake back over on a plate or another cake board.
20. Slice a cold cheesecake with a warmed chef's knife. Wipe the knife after each cut.

BROWNIE CUBES

INGREDIENTS

- 1 cup all-purpose flour
- 1/3 cup unsweetened cocoa powder sifted
- 1/2 teaspoon baking powder
- 1/2 teaspoon salt
- 2 cups granulated sugar
- 1 cup unsalted butter, melted and cooled to room temperature
- 2 teaspoons pure vanilla extract
- 4 eggs
- 2 cups semisweet chocolate chips

INSTRUCTIONS

1. Preheat the oven to 325 F. degrees.
2. Grease a 9 x 13 baking dish with cooking spray.
3. Cut a piece of parchment paper to fit on the bottom and sides of the pan. When the brownies cool, you can use the parchment paper to lift brownies from the pan. Spray with cooking spray.
4. Whisk the flour, cocoa powder, baking powder, and salt in a small bowl.
5. Mix the sugar, melted butter, and vanilla in a large bowl with an electric mixer.
6. Slowly add the eggs one at a time to the sugar and butter mixture, fully incorporating each egg before adding the next.
7. Turn the mixer to low and add the flour mixture until just combined.
8. Fold the chocolate chips into the batter with a large rubber spatula.
9. Pour the batter into the prepared dish and spread evenly.
10. Bake for 45 minutes until a cake tester or toothpick inserted into the center comes out with moist crumbs attached. Don't overcook the brownies. Bake between 165 F. to 180 F. degrees. 165 F. degrees if you like fudgy brownies.
11. Let them cool completely before cutting them into inch squares.
12. Refrigerate overnight, remove it from the pan, and stack the cube brownies on it.
13. Before serving, drizzle the chocolate sauce over the brownies.

EASY CHOCOLATE SAUCE

INGREDIENTS

- 3/4 cup semisweet chocolate, chopped
- 1 (14-ounce) can of sweetened condensed milk
- ¼ teaspoon salt
- 2 teaspoons pure vanilla extract
- 3 tablespoons butter

INSTRUCTIONS

1. In a heavy saucepan over low heat, melt the chocolate with the sweetened condensed milk.
2. Once the mixture is melts and is combined, stir in the salt, vanilla, and butter.
3. Allow it to cool slightly but still be pourable.
4. Drizzle the fudge over the brownies and cheesecake.

HOMEMADE BILLIONAIRE BROWNIES
with Chocolate Frosting

If I could only have one dessert, please give me these homemade brownies. I'll add vanilla ice cream to a warm brownie and drizzle hot fudge all over the top. Next, I sprinkle salted pecans over everything. This is my ultimate dessert. I wouldn't take a billion dollars for it which is why I call them my Billionaire Brownies. Brownie Recipe (See page 117)

CHOCOLATE BUTTERCREAM

INGREDIENTS

- 1 cup butter, softened
- 3 cups powdered sugar
- ⅔ cup cocoa powder sifted
- 2 teaspoons pure vanilla extract
- ¼ teaspoon salt
- ¼ cup heavy cream

INSTRUCTIONS

1. Using an electric mixer, beat the softened butter until creamy.
2. Slowly add the powdered sugar and cocoa.
3. Mix in the vanilla and salt.
4. Drizzle in the heavy cream.
5. Scrape down the sides and whip buttercream on high for 3 to 4 minutes.
6. When the brownies are cool, spread the frosting over them.
7. Just before serving, sprinkle salted pecans (See Page 64) over the frosting.

BOSTON CREAM MINI CHEESECAKES

These treats are the cutest, creamiest, sweet combination. They include a little homemade pudding and a dab of chocolate. The perfect treat.

GRAHAM CRACKER CRUST

INGREDIENTS

- 1-1/2 cup graham cracker crumbs
- 6 tablespoons butter, melted
- ¼ cup brown sugar

INSTRUCTIONS

1. Preheat the oven to 325 degrees F and line a regular muffin tin with cupcake liners.
2. Place the graham crackers in a food processor and process until fine crumbs. You can crush the cookies in a ziplock bag and use a mallet or rolling pin.
3. Add the melted butter and sugar to your crumbs and combine.
4. Divide evenly into the paper liners and press firmly using a spoon or glass.
5. Bake crust for 5 minutes.

CHEESECAKE

INGREDIENTS

- 2 (8-oz.) full-fat cream cheese, softened
- 3/4 cup sugar
- 1-1/2 teaspoon pure vanilla extract
- 2 large eggs
- 1/4 cup sour cream
- 2 tablespoons heavy cream

INSTRUCTIONS

1. Combine the cream cheese, sugar, and vanilla, until fluffy with an electric mixer.
2. Mix in the eggs one at a time until just combined.
3. Stir in the sour cream and heavy cream and mix until combined. Don't overmix.
4. Use an ice cream scoop and scoop even amounts of cheesecake filling on top of each graham cracker crust
5. Tap on the counter to release air bubbles.
6. Bake cheesecakes for 20 minutes at 325 F. degrees or until the filling is almost set. The center will giggle slightly.
7. Cool completely.

VANILLA PUDDING

INGREDIENTS

- 4 egg yolks
- 1/4 cup cornstarch
- 1/8 teaspoon salt
- 2 cups half-and-half
- 3/4 cup sugar
- 2 teaspoons vanilla paste
- 2 tablespoons butter
- ½ cup heavy cream

INSTRUCTIONS

1. Heat half-and-half and sugar in the microwave for 3 to 4 minutes. The milk should be steaming but not boiling. Stir the mixture carefully. It may have air bubbles.
2. In a separate bowl, whisk egg yolks until a pale-yellow color. Whisk in cornstarch and salt with the egg yolks. Once the egg yolks and cornstarch are light and smooth, it's ready for the half-and-half.
3. Slowly drizzle a cup of the warm milk over the egg mixture while constantly whisking. Use one hand to drizzle the milk into the egg yolks and one hand to whisk the mixture. Place a silicone mat or a towel under your bowl to prevent it from slipping. Whisk in the remaining warm milk.
4. Pour the mixture into a clean pot and whisk over medium heat until it thickens.
5. Cook while whisking until the pudding starts bubbling and is thick. Be sure to whisk in the corners of the pot. Use a silicone spatula to clean the sides of the pot periodically. The custard will burn if left on the sides.
6. Remove from the heat at 175 to 180 F. degrees. After coating the back of a spoon and swiping your finger through the custard, it should remain separated.
7. Add butter and vanilla paste and whisk until the butter melts and is incorporated.
8. Put the pudding in a container to cool.
9. Press a piece of plastic wrap onto the surface of the pudding to prevent skin from forming. Let it cool at room temperature before placing it in the pie crust.
10. When ready to serve, whip the heavy cream until stiff peaks form and fold it into the pudding.
11. Pipe or place one to two tablespoons of pudding on each cheesecake and refrigerate while making the buttercream.
12. Pipe the chocolate buttercream on top of each cheesecake.

CHOCOLATE BUTTERCREAM

INGREDIENTS

- 1 cup butter, softened
- 3 cups powdered sugar
- ⅔ cup cocoa powder sifted
- 2 teaspoons pure vanilla extract
- ¼ teaspoon salt
- ¼ cup heavy cream

INSTRUCTIONS

1. Using an electric mixer, beat the softened butter until creamy.
2. Slowly add the powdered sugar and cocoa.
3. Mix in the vanilla and salt.
4. Drizzle in the heavy cream.
5. Scrape down the sides and whip buttercream on high for 3 to 4 minutes.

BOSTON CREAM PIE COOKIES

You'll love the crunchy cookie with the creamy pudding and chocolate. It's a classic combination with a little crunch.

COOKIE CUPS

INGREDIENTS

- 1 cup butter softened
- 1-1/2 cups sugar
- 2 eggs
- 3 teaspoons pure vanilla extract
- 2-3/4 cups of all-purpose flour
- 1 teaspoon baking powder
- 1/2 teaspoon salt
- ½ cup chocolate chips melted

INSTRUCTIONS

1. Preheat oven to 350 degrees. Spray two regular-size muffin tins with cooking spray.
2. Cream the butter and sugar until fluffy in a stand mixer.
3. Add the eggs one at a time and continue beating until incorporated.
4. Mix in the vanilla.
5. Whisk together the flour, baking powder, and salt.
6. Add them to the butter and sugar mixture just until combined.
7. Use a regular ice cream scoop (3 tablespoons), and scoop dough into muffin tins.
8. Bake for 12 minutes. The edges will be slightly golden.
9. Remove from the oven.
10. Use a tablespoon or a small round lid to press an indention in the middle of each cookie. (A glass spice jar works well.)
11. Melt the chocolate chips in the microwave for 15 seconds and stir until creamy.
12. Brush the melted chocolate in the hot cookie cups.
13. Cool for ten minutes in the pan.
14. Remove from the pan and cool completely on a large baking sheet.

TIP

The melted chocolate acts as a barrier to keep the cookie cups from getting soggy. Best if eaten on the same day.

VANILLA PUDDING

INGREDIENTS

- 4 egg yolks
- 1/4 cup cornstarch
- 1/8 teaspoon salt
- 2 cups half-and-half
- 3/4 cup sugar
- 2 teaspoons vanilla paste
- 2 tablespoons butter
- ½ cup heavy cream

INSTRUCTIONS

1. Heat half-and-half and sugar in the microwave for 3 to 4 minutes. The milk should be steaming but not boiling. Stir the mixture carefully. It may have air bubbles.
2. In a separate bowl, whisk egg yolks until a pale-yellow color. Whisk in cornstarch and salt with the egg yolks. Once the egg yolks and cornstarch are light and smooth, it's ready for the half-and-half.
3. Slowly drizzle a cup of the warm milk over the egg mixture while constantly whisking. Use one hand to drizzle the milk into the egg yolks and one hand to whisk the mixture. Place a silicone mat or a towel under your bowl to prevent it from slipping. Whisk in the remaining warm milk.
4. Pour the mixture into a clean pot and whisk over medium heat until it thickens.
5. Cook while whisking until the pudding starts bubbling and is thick. Be sure to whisk in the corners of the pot. Use a silicone spatula to clean the sides of the pot periodically. The custard will burn if left on the sides.
6. Remove from the heat at 175 to 180 F. degrees. After coating the back of a spoon and swiping your finger through the custard, it should remain separated.
7. Add butter and vanilla and whisk until the butter is melted and incorporated.
8. Press a piece of plastic wrap onto the surface of the pudding to prevent skin from forming. Let it cool at room temperature.
9. When ready to serve, whip the heavy cream and fold it into the pudding.
10. Pipe or spoon the pudding into the cookie cups and refrigerate while making the buttercream.
11. Pipe chocolate buttercream on the pudding.

CHOCOLATE BUTTERCREAM

INGREDIENTS

- 1 cup butter, softened
- 3 cups powdered sugar
- ⅔ cup cocoa powder sifted
- 2 teaspoons pure vanilla extract
- ¼ teaspoon salt
- ¼ cup heavy cream

INSTRUCTIONS

1. Using an electric mixer, beat the softened butter until creamy.
2. Slowly add the powdered sugar and cocoa.
3. Mix in the vanilla and salt.
4. Drizzle in the heavy cream.
5. Scrape down the sides and whip buttercream on high for 3 to 4 minutes.

WHITE CHOCOLATE BREAD PUDDING

While living in the New Orleans area, I fell in love with White Chocolate Bread Pudding after my first bite. I had to learn how to make it. I elevate this fabulous White Chocolate Bread Pudding with white chocolate sauce and berry sauce. The slight tartness of the berries is the perfect combination with the sweet white chocolate.

Bread pudding can easily be overcooked and become dry. Even if an over-baked bread pudding includes a sauce, it can be almost impossible to cover up the dryness. I added an internal temperature to prevent this problem. Once it reaches the ideal temperature, remove it from the oven for a perfectly cooked bread pudding.

INGREDIENTS

- French Bread loaf sliced into 1-inch cubes, about 5 cups
- 12 ounces of white chocolate
- One cup of whole milk
- 3 cups heavy cream
- 1/2 cup granulated sugar
- 8 egg yolks
- 2 whole eggs
- 2 teaspoons pure vanilla extract
- ½ teaspoon salt

INSTRUCTIONS

1. Preheat the oven to 275 F. degrees.
2. Bake the French bread on a baking sheet in the oven for 15 minutes to help dry it out.
3. Heat heavy cream, milk, and sugar in the microwave just until steaming, about four minutes.
4. Remove from the heat and add the white chocolate. Stir until the chocolate melts completely.
5. In a separate bowl, beat the eggs and egg yolks until light and fluffy.
6. Drizzle two cups of warm cream while whisking into the egg mixture. Whisk the rest of the warm cream into the eggs.
7. Add the pure vanilla extract and salt.
8. Layer half of the bread into a deep 9 x 13 baking pan
9. Pour the custard over the bread and allow a few minutes for the bread to soak up all the custard. Press the bread down.
10. Cover with aluminum foil and bake at 275 F. degrees for 1 hour. Test the temperature with an instant-read thermometer.
11. Remove the foil from the bread pudding and continue baking.
12. Remove from the oven when it reaches 160 F.-165 F. degrees internal temperature.
13. Cool to room temperature.
14. To serve, cut into squares and place on serving plates.
15. Warm the sauces in mason jars for a minute in the microwave.
16. Drizzle with warm White Chocolate Sauce and Berry Sauce.

WHITE CHOCOLATE SAUCE

INGREDIENTS

- 1 cup of white chocolate
- 1/3 cup heavy cream

INSTRUCTIONS

1. Heat the cream and chocolate in the microwave for one minute and stir well until smooth. It may need another thirty seconds in the microwave.

BERRY COMPOTE

INGREDIENTS

- 4 cups mixed berries
- 3/4 cup sugar
- ¼ cup fresh orange juice
- Zest from large orange

INSTRUCTIONS

1. Add all ingredients to a medium size pot.
2. Cook until berries break down and juices are released, 10 to 15 minutes.
3. Strain through a fine mesh strainer to remove skin and seeds. If you don't mind the skin and seeds, skip this step. You could also use your food processor or an immersion blender to get rid of the skin and seeds.

WHITE CHOCOLATE CRÈME BRULEE

If you're looking for a fancy delicious dessert, here it is. This white chocolate creme brulee is a fabulous recipe. I learned how to make it while living in the New Orleans area. The white chocolate in this creme brulee makes your mouth happy. It's worth the extra effort to prepare it. Use a blow torch for the crunchy topping. You can also place it under the oven broiler. Elevate it with a dollop of homemade whipped cream and a few fresh berries. The tartness of the berries is perfect with the sweet custard. The berries also add color.

INGREDIENTS

- 6 large eggs yolks
- 2-1/2 cups heavy cream
- 1/2 cup sugar
- 1 cup white chocolate chips
- 2 teaspoons vanilla paste
- 3 tablespoons granulated sugar mixed with 3 tablespoons brown sugar for the brulee.

INSTRUCTIONS

1. Preheat oven to 325 F. degrees.
2. In a large microwave bowl, (glass measuring cup), bring the heavy cream, sugar, white chocolate, and vanilla paste to steaming but not boiling.
3. In a medium bowl, whisk the egg yolks until light and creamy.
4. Whisk two cups of the heated cream mixture slowly into the egg yolks.
5. Whisk in the remaining cream mixture.
6. Pour the mixture through a fine mesh sieve.
7. Divide it into eight 4-ounce ramekins.
8. Put the ramekins in a large pan and fill it with hot water to come halfway up the sides of the ramekins.
9. Bake for 25 to 30 minutes or until set. They should have a slight giggle in the center. An internal temperature should read 170 -175 F. degrees.
10. Remove from the oven and the water bath. Cool to room temperature.
11. Cover with plastic wrap and refrigerate overnight if possible or until very cold.
12. When ready to serve, sprinkle the top of the custards with the sugar/brown sugar combination.
13. Caramelize the sugar with a kitchen blowtorch or place the custards in a pan of ice water and broil until the tops are caramelized. Watch them carefully.
14. As the sugar crust cools, it will harden.
15. Serve with Homemade Whipped Cream and fresh berries.

EASIEST CHOCOLATE PIE
with Marshmallow Whipped Cream

This easy two-ingredient chocolate pie is elevated with sweet marshmallow whipped cream. Marshmallows and chocolate are the perfect combinations to elevate this simple pie.

CHOCOLATE PIE

INGREDIENTS

- 9" pie crust already baked, or a graham cracker crust.
- 1 cup chocolate, chopped (milk, semi-sweet, or dark).
- 1 (8 oz.) frozen whipped topping, thawed.

INSTRUCTIONS

1. Bake the pie crust and cool completely.
2. In a large microwave bowl, microwave the chocolate for a minute.
3. Whisk until completely smooth and creamy.
4. Let cool for two minutes.
5. Fold in the whipped topping.
6. Smooth out the pie crust.
7. Refrigerate overnight.
8. Spread the marshmallow whipped cream on top of the pie.
9. Grate chocolate over the whipped cream.

MARSHMALLOW WHIPPED CREAM

INGREDIENTS

- 1 cup heavy whipping cream, cold
- 7 tablespoons of Marshmallow Fluff or Marshmallow Cream
- 1 teaspoon vanilla extract
- ¼ teaspoon salt

INSTRUCTIONS

1. Using an electric mixer, beat cold heavy whipping cream until stiff peaks.
2. Add marshmallow cream, vanilla, and salt.
3. Scrape down the sides of the mixer, and mix until blended.

CREAMY CITRUS DESSERTS
A Little Bit of Sunshine

This chapter includes Key Lime and Lemon desserts. Your taste buds will dance as you experience these tart, tangy, but sweet combinations. They are all light, refreshing, and packed with flavor. You'll find both easy and made-from-scratch citrus recipes.

After my father passed, I purchased several orange, lemon, and key lime trees to remember him. He grew up in an orange grove in Florida. In Arkansas, I had to grow them in pots, but they are full of citrus every year and smell amazing. They are my favorite thing to use in my desserts.

GINGERSNAP KEY LIME PIE
with Homemade Whipped Cream and Raspberry Sauce

Even though this sweet and tangy treat is baked, it is easy to make. It is elevated with homemade whipped cream, raspberry sauce, plus a delicious gingersnap crust.

GINGERSNAP CRUST

INGREDIENTS

- 1-1/2 cups gingersnap crumbs
- 1/4 cup brown sugar
- 6 tablespoons butter, melted

INSTRUCTIONS

1. Process the gingersnap cookies in the food processor to make fine crumbs. You can also use a ziplock bag.
2. Transfer to a bowl and stir in the brown sugar and butter.
3. Press into a 9-inch deep dish pie crust.

KEY LIME PIE FILLING

INGREDIENTS

- 6 large egg yolks
- Zest of 2 limes
- 2 (14-ounce) cans of sweetened condensed milk
- 1 cup key fresh lime juice or Nellie & Joe's Famous Key Lime Juice

INSTRUCTIONS

1. Whisk the egg yolks and zest until pale and fluffy.
2. Slowly add the sweetened condensed milk until the mixture is smooth and thick.
3. Add the key lime juice and beat just until combined.
4. Bake at 325 degrees for 18-22 minutes. It should still jiggle a little in the center but not look wet. The internal temperature should be 145 F. degrees.
5. Cool completely and refrigerate for two to four hours before serving.

WHIPPED TOPPING

INGREDIENTS

- 1/1-2 cups heavy cream
- 3/4 cup confectioners' sugar
- 1 tablespoon lime juice
- Zest of 2 limes
- 1/4 cup toasted coconut

INSTRUCTIONS

1. Whip heavy cream and powdered sugar until stiff. Add key lime juice just until incorporated.
2. Use a piping bag and a 1M tip to pipe swirls of cream. Add the zested lime and toasted coconut over the top of the whipped cream.

RASPBERRY SAUCE

INGREDIENTS

- 2 cups fresh raspberries
- Juice of one lemon
- 1/3 cup sugar

INSTRUCTIONS

1. Add all the ingredients to a saucepan and cook over medium heat until thick, for 10 to 15 minutes.
2. Strain the raspberry sauce and chill.

NO-BAKE GINGERSNAP KEY LIME
Cheesecake Pie

GINGERSNAP CRUST

INGREDIENTS

- 1-1/2 cups gingersnap crumbs
- ¼ cup brown sugar
- 6 tablespoons butter, melted

INSTRUCTIONS

1. Process the gingersnap cookies in the food processor to make fine crumbs. You can also use a ziplock bag.
2. Transfer to a bowl and stir in the brown sugar and butter.
3. Press into a 9-pie dish.
4. Bake 350 F degrees for 12 minutes.

KEY LIME CHEESECAKE FILLING

INGREDIENTS

- 1 (8 ounces) cream cheese softened
- 1 can of sweetened condensed milk
- 1/2 cup fresh key lime juice or Nellie & Joe's Famous Key Lime Juice
- 1 lime, zested
- 1 teaspoon coconut extract
- 12 ounces frozen whipped topping, thawed

INSTRUCTIONS

1. Use an electric mixer and cream the cream cheese and sweetened condensed milk.
2. Mix in key lime juice, lime zest, and coconut extract.
3. Fold in two cups of thawed whipped topping.
4. Place pie ingredients in graham cracker crust.
5. Top with the remaining whipped cream.
6. Refrigerate for four hours or overnight for best results.
7. Garnish with lime slices and lime zest.

KEY LIME BARS
with White Chocolate

Here is the perfect crowd-pleaser for a summer gathering. The white chocolate goes perfectly with the tangy key lime.

SPICED CRUST

INGREDIENTS

- 3-1/2 cups graham cracker crumbs
- 1/2 cup brown sugar
- 1 tablespoon pumpkin pie spice
- 12 tablespoons butter, melted

INSTRUCTIONS

1. Process the graham crackers in the food processor to make fine crumbs. You can also use a ziplock bag.
2. Transfer to a bowl and stir in the brown sugar, pumpkin pie spice, and butter.
3. Use the bottom of a glass and press the crumbs into a 15 x 10-inch jelly roll sheet pan.
4. Bake 350 F degrees for 10 minutes.

FILLING

INGREDIENTS

- 9 large egg yolks
- 2 tablespoons fresh lime zest
- 3 (14-ounce) cans of sweetened condensed milk
- 1-1/2 cup key lime juice, Nellie & Joe's Famous Key Lime Juice

INSTRUCTIONS

1. Whisk the egg yolks and zest until pale and fluffy with an electric mixer.
2. Slowly add the sweetened condensed milk until the mixture is smooth and thick.
3. Add the key lime juice and beat just until combined.
4. Bake 325 degrees for 13-15 minutes or until the center sets. The internal temperature should be 145 F. degrees.
5. Cool at room temperature.

TOPPING

INGREDIENTS

- 1 cup white chocolate chips
- 1/3 cup heavy cream

INSTRUCTIONS

1. Heat the heavy cream and white chocolate in the microwave for about a minute.
2. Stir continuously until the chocolate is smooth.
3. Cool the chocolate to room temperature before pouring over the key lime bars.
4. Drizzle the chocolate over the bars.
5. Refrigerate until firm.

EASIEST LEMONADE PIE

With Berry Sauce

I had to include this super easy lemonade pie in this chapter. It's in remembrance of my father-in-law, Don. He loved it. To elevate this pie, I add a delicious berry sauce. This pie is fabulous frozen as well.

FILLING

INGREDIENTS

- Graham cracker pie crust
- 1 (14-ounce) can sweetened condensed milk
- 1 (6-ounce) can of frozen lemonade, partially thawed
- 1 (8-ounce container) frozen whipped topping, thawed

INSTRUCTIONS

1. Stir by hand the condensed milk and lemonade concentrate in a large bowl until smooth.
2. Fold in the whipped topping.
3. Pour into a graham cracker crust and freeze for 4 hours or until firm.
4. Serve with a berry compote and homemade whipped cream (page 128).

TIP

This pie can be refrigerated instead of freezing for a softer texture. Substitute 6-ounce frozen lemonade concentrate for 6 ounces of pink lemonade concentrate. Serve mini muffin size for a party with the whipped heavy cream.

BERRY SAUCE

INGREDIENTS

- 4 cups mixed berries
- 1/2 cup sugar
- ¼ cup fresh lemon juice
- Zest from large lemon

INSTRUCTIONS

1. Add all ingredients to a medium size pot.
2. Cook until berries break down and juices are released, 10 to 15 minutes.
3. Strain through a fine mesh strainer to remove skin and seeds.
4. If you don't mind the skin and seeds, skip this step. You could also use your food processor or an immersion blender to get rid of the skin and seeds.

EASY NO BAKE LEMON CHEESECAKE PIE
with Blueberry Whipped Cream

Here is another super easy creamy sweet but tart pie with only five ingredients. I elevate it with blueberry whipped cream. It's easy to make using freeze-dried blueberries and packed with blueberry flavor.

INGREDIENTS

- 1 (9") graham cracker crust
- 8 oz. cream cheese (room temperature)
- 1 (14 oz.) can of sweetened condensed milk
- ½ cup fresh lemon juice
- zest of two lemons

INSTRUCTIONS

1. Place the cream cheese into a mixing bowl and use an electric mixer to blend until smooth and creamy. Add the sweetened condensed milk, lemon juice, and lemon zest and blend until the ingredients are fully incorporated and completely smooth.
2. Pour the filling into the pre-made graham cracker pie crust, smooth the top, and chill in the refrigerator for 2 hours to set.
3. Mound homemade blueberry whipped cream on the pie for a beautiful presentation.
4. Zest a couple of lemons over the whipped cream.

TIP

Elevate this pie by layering it in individual glasses with a graham cracker crust, lemon cream cheese filling, and berry sauce withhomemade whipped cream.

DECORATE WITH BLUEBERRY WHIPPED CREAM

INGREDIENTS

- 1-1/2 cups heavy cream
- Freeze-dried blueberries, 4 tablespoons of powder
- 3/4 cup confectioners' sugar

INSTRUCTIONS

1. Add the freeze-dried berries to a food processor. Pulse into powder.
2. Whip the heavy cream, blueberry powder, and powdered sugar until stiff peaks form. The extra powdered sugar helps stabilize the whipped cream.
3. Use a pastry bag fitted with a #1M, 9FT, or #1C tip, and hold the bag vertically above the pie on the outer edge.
4. Place the tip slightly above the pie and apply pressure. As you pipe, slowly lift the bag and make two small dollops on top of each other before releasing pressure and pulling up. Do this around the pie.

LEMON ICE BOX PIE
with Coconut Whipped Cream

Who doesn't love lemon icebox pie? It's creamy, tart, and fabulous! Lemon and coconut were made for each other which is why I elevate this pie with homemade coconut whipped cream topped with toasted coconut.

INGREDIENTS

- 2 cans of sweetened condensed milk
- 1 cup lemon juice, freshly squeezed (about 6 large lemons)
- 6 egg yolks
- 1 tablespoon lemon zest
- 1 (9-inch) deep dish spiced graham-cracker pie crust (See page 132)

INSTRUCTIONS

1. Preheat the oven to 325 degrees.
2. Combine the condensed milk, lemon juice, and egg yolks on medium speed for at least ten minutes.
3. Pour into the pie shell and bake for 20 minutes.
4. Remove from the oven at around an internal temperature of 145 F. degrees.
5. Cool to room temperature.
6. Refrigerate for at least four hours.
7. Using a piping bag or ziplock bag fitted with a 1M or 2D tip, pipe swirls of whipped cream on the edge of the pie.
8. Add a slice of lemon to each swirl.
9. When plating, add a spoonful of berry sauce to the side of the plate.
10. Use the back of a spoon, and place it in the center of the sauce.
11. Drag the spoon down to pull the sauce across the plate.
12. Garnish the plate and pie with coconut whipped cream.

COCONUT WHIPPED CREAM

INGREDIENTS

- 2 cups heavy cream
- ¾ cup powdered sugar
- 2 teaspoons coconut extract
- ¼ cup toasted coconut

INSTRUCTIONS

1. Whip the heavy cream and powdered sugar until stiff.
2. Add the coconut extract.
3. Mound the coconut whipped cream on top of the lemon pie.
4. Sprinkle the toasted coconut on top of the whipped cream.

MINI LEMON CURD CHEESECAKES

What is my favorite way to eat lemon curd? I like it on a spoon straight out of a bowl. The sweet, tart, light, and creamy goodness is amazing. What makes it even better is making it quick and easy in the microwave. These cute mini cheesecakes are elevated with my microwave lemon curd. The lemon curd and the cheesecakes are best if made a few days in advance.

GRAHAM CRACKER CRUST

INGREDIENTS

- 1-1/2 cup graham cracker crumbs
- 6 tablespoons butter, melted
- 1/4 cup brown sugar

INSTRUCTIONS

1. Preheat the oven to 325 F. degrees.
2. Use a 12-cup mini cheesecake pan with removable bottoms or a 12-cup regular muffin tin. Use cupcake liners with the muffin tin. Spray pans with baking spray.
3. Place the graham crackers in a food processor and process until fine crumbs or crush the crackers in a ziplock bag using a mallet or rolling pin.
4. Combine the melted butter and brown sugar to your crumbs.
5. Evenly distribute the crumb mixture between the bottom of each cupcake liner and press down using a tablespoon or small glass.
6. Bake the crust for 6 minutes.
7. Cool to room temperature.

CHEESECAKE FILLING

INGREDIENTS

- 2 (8-oz.) full-fat cream cheese, softened
- 3/4 cup sugar
- 1-1/2 teaspoons pure vanilla extract
- 1 tablespoon lemon zest
- 3 tablespoons fresh lemon juice
- 2 large eggs
- 1/4 cup sour cream

INSTRUCTIONS

1. Using an electric mixer, cream the cream cheese, sugar, vanilla, lemon zest, and lemon juice until fluffy.
2. Mix in the eggs one at a time until just combined.
3. Stir in the sour cream and mix until combined. Don't over-mix.
4. Use an ice cream scoop and scoop even amounts of cheesecake filling on top of each graham cracker crust.
5. Tap on the counter to release air bubbles.
6. Bake cheesecakes for 20 minutes or until the filling sets. The center will be giggling slightly. The internal temperature should be around 150 F. degrees.
7. Cool completely and refrigerate for a couple of hours.
8. When serving, add a tablespoon of lemon curd to each cheesecake and top with homemade whipped cream.

MICROWAVE LEMON CURD

INGREDIENTS

- 1 cup sugar
- 2 lemons zested
- 1/2 cup of fresh lemon juice
- 6 egg yolks
- ½ cup butter, cold, cubed

INSTRUCTIONS

1. In a microwave-safe bowl, combine the sugar and lemon zest. Use a fork and press the zest into the sugar.
2. Whisk in the lemon juice and egg yolk.
3. Microwave on high for one minute and stir. Continue microwaving for one minute and stirring after each minute until the lemon curd coats the back of a spoon, 3 to 5 minutes.
4. Remove the curd from the microwave. The internal temperature should be 175 F. degrees.
5. Add a few tablespoons of cold butter at a time.
6. Stir until fully incorporated.
7. Pour into mason jars. Let cool completely and refrigerate. It will thicken as it cools.

LEMON CHESS PIE
with Strawberry Whipped Cream

If you enjoy a comforting chess pie, you will love this Lemon Chess Pie. I elevated it with strawberry whipped cream using freeze-dried strawberries. Use a food processor, pulse the freeze-dried strawberries into powder, and add them to the whipped cream. The whipped cream is incredibly flavorful.

LEMON CHESS PIE

INGREDIENTS

- 2 cups sugar
- 1 tablespoon all-purpose flour
- 2 tablespoons yellow cornmeal
- 1/4 teaspoon salt
- 4 egg yolks, beaten
- 1/4 cup butter, melted
- 1/4 cup buttermilk
- 1/4 cup lemon juice, fresh
- 1 tablespoon lemon zest
- 1 teaspoon vanilla
- 1 pie crust, baked for 10 minutes

INSTRUCTIONS

1. Preheat oven to 350 F. degrees.
2. Combine sugar, flour, cornmeal, and salt using a whisk.
3. Add remaining ingredients.
4. Use an electric mixer and continue beating until thick, 3 - 5 minutes.
5. Bake at 350 F. degrees for 45 minutes or until the filling sets in the center. If necessary, cover with aluminum foil for the last few minutes to prevent excessive browning.
6. The internal temperature should be around 190 F. degrees.
7. Cool completely before decorating the pie with strawberry whipped cream.

STRAWBERRY WHIPPED CREAM

INGREDIENTS

- 1-1/2 cups heavy cream
- Freeze-dried strawberries, 4 tablespoons of powder
- 3/4 cup confectioners' sugar

INSTRUCTIONS

1. Add the freeze-dried strawberries to a food processor. Pulse into powder.
2. Whip the heavy cream, strawberry powder, and powdered sugar until stiff peaks form. The extra powdered sugar helps stabilize the whipped cream.
3. Use a pastry bag fitted with a #1M tip.
4. Hold the bag vertically above the pie on the outer edge. Place the tip slightly above the pie and apply pressure. As you pipe, slowly lift the bag and make two small swirls on top of each other before releasing pressure and pulling up. Do this around the pie.

CREAMY PEANUT BUTTER DESSERTS

This chapter is short with only two super easy recipes. These are still two of my most requested desserts. The peanut butter pie and the peanut butter balls are delicious on their own, but to elevate the pie, I stack the peanut butter balls high on top of it. Drizzle the peanut butter balls with any color of candy melts or sprinkles to coordinate with the season or any party theme.

PEANUT BUTTER PIE NO BAKE

CHOCOLATE CRUST

INGREDIENTS

- 26 Chocolate sandwich cookies with a white filling.
- 6 tablespoons butter

INSTRUCTIONS

1. Use a food processor to crush the chocolate sandwich cookies.
2. Add the butter.
3. Press into a 9-inch deep dish pie pan.
4. Bake 350 degrees for 12-15 minutes. Completely cool.

PEANUT BUTTER PIE FILLING

INGREDIENTS

- 1-1/4 cups peanut butter
- 8 ounces of cream cheese
- 1 cup confectioners' sugar
- 1 (8 oz) container of frozen whipped topping, thawed
- 1 cup of mini chocolate chips

INSTRUCTIONS

1. Using an electric mixer, cream together the peanut butter and cream cheese.
2. Slowly mix in the confectioner's sugar.
3. Fold the thawed whipped topping into the peanut butter mixture.
4. Stir in the mini chocolate chips.
5. Place the peanut butter filling in the cooled prepared pie crust. It will be full.
6. Allow this pie to chill in the refrigerator overnight. It needs to be completely firm before stacking the peanut butter balls.

TIP

For an easier version, stack peanut butter cups on top of the pie and drizzle with fudge.

NO BAKE PEANUT BUTTER BALLS

Decorate your peanut butter pie by piling these delicious peanut butter balls on top of it. Add color to the pie to go with any theme, by drizzling melted candy melts over the chocolate or colorful sprinkles.

INGREDIENTS

- 2 cups creamy peanut butter
- 1 cup butter, softened
- 1 tablespoon vanilla
- ¼ teaspoon salt
- 4 cups powdered sugar
- 1 package (10 oz) melting chocolate (Ghirardelli)
- 1 cup of candy melts or sprinkles, any color

INSTRUCTIONS

1. Mix peanut butter, butter, vanilla, and salt using an electric mixer until blended.
2. Gradually add powdered sugar.
3. Use a rubber spatula to combine and press them together.
4. Shape into one-inch balls and freeze for twenty minutes. A tablespoon ice cream scoop works well.
5. Place in the freezer for thirty minutes.
6. Melt the chocolate according to the package directions in the microwave.
7. Using a toothpick or fork, dip each ball halfway in the chocolate and place it on parchment paper to harden with the chocolate side up. The chocolate will harden in a few minutes.
8. When the chocolate sets, drizzle melted candy melts over the tops.
9. Add sprinkles before the chocolate sets or before the candy melts set.

CREAMY TROPICAL DESSERTS

This chapter is full of creamy, dreamy coconut and pineapple recipes. Tropical desserts are light, refreshing, and the perfect way to end a summer meal. Hopefully, one bite of these desserts will transport you to a tropical paradise.

COCONUT PRALINE CREAM PIE

My husband loves coconut cream pies. Before I started making coconut pies from scratch, I used this recipe. To elevate it, I added a crunchy praline layer. It's easy to make and delicious.

PRALINE LAYER

This praline layer is fabulous in coconut pie but goes well in many pies. It will harden as it cools in the pie crust. Let it completely cool before adding the filling.

INGREDIENTS

- 1/2 cup pecans, chopped
- 3 tablespoons butter
- 1/3 cup brown sugar
- 1/8 teaspoon salt
- 1-9-inch-deep dish pie crust, baked and cooled. (See Page 14)

INSTRUCTIONS

1. Heat pecans, butter, brown sugar, and salt in a small saucepan until the butter and sugar have dissolved and the mixture begins to boil.
2. Boil and stir continuously for 30 seconds, then remove from heat.
3. Add the praline sauce to the bottom of the prebaked deep dish pie crust.
4. Once you put the praline sauce in the pie crust, let it Cool completely before adding the pudding.

COCONUT FILLING

INGREDIENTS

- 2 cups whole milk
- 2 (3.4-ounce) boxes of instant coconut cream pudding mix or vanilla pudding
- 1 (14 oz) sweetened condensed milk
- 8 ounces of cream cheese
- 1 teaspoon pure vanilla extract
- 1 teaspoon coconut extract
- 1-1/2 cups coconut
- 12-ounce container of frozen whipped topping, thawed
- 1/4 cup toasted coconut

INSTRUCTIONS

1. Mix the milk and pudding until well combined.
2. In a separate bowl, whip the sweetened condensed milk, cream cheese, vanilla extract, and coconut extract, and continue blending until well combined.
3. Fold in the pudding.
4. Fold two cups of whipped topping and the coconut into the pudding mixture.
5. Spread the mixture into the pie crust.
6. Mound the rest of the whipped topping on top of the pudding. It'll be very full.
7. Sprinkle it with toasted coconut.

TOASTED COCONUT RECIPE

INGREDIENTS

- 1/4 cup coconut

INSTRUCTIONS

1. Spread coconut on a baking sheet and bake at 350 F. degrees for 10 to 15 minutes. Watch the coconut closely. Don't let it burn.

MADE-FROM-SCRATCH COCONUT PRALINE CREAM PIE
with Homemade Whipped Cream

This made-from-scratch Praline Coconut Cream Pie has been made hundreds of times in my house. It's my husband's favorite pie and my most requested one. I keep the supplies on hand to surprise friends and family for special occasions.

Pie crust – One baked and cooled deep dish pie crust - Perfect Pie Crust (See page 14)

PRALINE LAYER

This praline layer is fabulous in coconut pie but goes well in many pies. It will harden as it cools in the pie crust.

INGREDIENTS

- 3 tablespoons butter
- 1/3 cup brown sugar
- 1/2 cup pecans
- 1/8 teaspoon salt

INSTRUCTIONS

1. Heat pecans, butter, brown sugar, and salt in a small saucepan until the butter and sugar have dissolved and the mixture begins to boil.
2. Stir continuously for 30-45 more seconds, then remove from heat.
3. Add the praline sauce to the bottom of the prebaked pie crust.
4. Once you put the praline sauce in the pie crust, let it Cool completely before adding the pastry cream.

COCONUT PUDDING

INGREDIENTS

- 3 cups half-and-half
- 3 cups coconut, divided
- 1-1/2 cups sugar
- 1/3 cup cornstarch
- 6 Egg yolks
- 1/4 teaspoon salt
- 2 teaspoons coconut flavoring
- 2 teaspoons pure vanilla extract
- 3 tablespoons unsalted butter

INSTRUCTIONS

1. Heat half-and-half, sugar, and two cups of coconut in the microwave for four minutes of full power to steam the milk. If not steaming, continue heating for thirty seconds at a time. Be extremely careful not to boil it. Stir the milk and sugar before and after heating it.
2. Microwave the remaining cup of coconut for thirty seconds in the microwave. The oils should begin to release.
3. Whisk egg yolks until a pale-yellow color. Whisk in cornstarch and salt with the egg yolks. Once the egg yolks and cornstarch are light and smooth, it's ready for the warm half-and-half.
4. Temper the eggs. Place a silicone mat or a towel under your bowl to prevent it from slipping. Slowly drizzle a cup of the warm milk over the egg mixture while constantly whisking. Use one hand to drizzle the milk into the egg yolks and one hand to whisk the mixture. Whisk in the remaining warm milk.
5. Pour the mixture into a large clean pot and whisk over medium heat until it thickens.
6. Cook while constantly whisking until the pudding is thick. Be sure to whisk in the corners of the pot. Use a silicone spatula to clean the sides of the pot. The custard will easily burn if left on the sides.
7. Once it starts boiling, use a thermometer to check the temperature.
8. Remove from the heat when it reaches 175 F. - 180 F. degrees. Don't go over 180 degrees.
9. It should coat the back of a spoon.
10. When you swipe your finger through the custard it should remain separated.
11. Add butter, coconut extract, and pure vanilla extract.
12. Whisk until the butter is completely melted and incorporated.
13. Stir the remaining coconut into the pudding.
14. Put the pudding into a bowl with plastic wrap on the surface to prevent skin from forming.
15. Let it cool at room temperature before placing it in the pie crust.

COCONUT WHIPPED CREAM

INGREDIENTS

- 1-1/2 cups heavy whipping cream
- 3/4 cup powdered sugar
- 2 teaspoons of coconut extract
- 1 teaspoon pure vanilla extract

INSTRUCTIONS

1. Whip the cream until foamy.
2. Gradually add the powdered sugar while continuing to beat.
3. Add the coconut extract and pure vanilla extract.
4. Beat until stiff peaks form.
5. Pile or pipe whipped cream over the pie filling. A 1M pastry tip was used in the picture to make the swirls.
6. Sprinkle it with toasted coconut.

TOASTED COCONUT RECIPE

INGREDIENTS

- 1/4 cup coconut

INSTRUCTIONS

1. Spread coconut on a baking sheet and bake at 350 F. degrees for about 5 minutes. Watch the coconut very closely. Don't let it burn.

BUTTERMILK PIE
with Coconut Whipped Cream

Don't knock it until you try it. I promise it doesn't taste like buttermilk. You'll love this creamy, tangy sweet pie. To elevate one of my favorite treats, I add homemade coconut whipped cream.

INGREDIENTS

- 1/2 cup butter, melted
- 2 cups sugar
- 3 tablespoons flour
- 4 eggs
- 1 cup buttermilk
- 2 teaspoons pure vanilla
- 1/2 teaspoon cinnamon
- 1/8 teaspoon salt
- unbaked pie crust
- Nutmeg

INSTRUCTIONS

1. Preheat the oven to 350 F. degrees.
2. Melt butter, add sugar, and flour, and beat well using an electric mixer.
3. Beat in eggs one at a time.
4. Add buttermilk, vanilla, cinnamon, and salt.
5. Pour mixture into an unbaked pie shell and sprinkle with nutmeg.
6. Bake 350 F. degrees and cook for 60 minutes or until the filling sets in the center. If necessary, cover with aluminum foil for the last few minutes to prevent excessive browning.
7. The internal temperature should reach 180 F. degrees.
8. Cool completely before decorating with coconut whipped cream or serve the whipped cream on the side when plating.

COCONUT WHIPPED CREAM

INGREDIENTS

- 1-1/2 cup heavy whipping cream
- 1/2 cup powdered sugar
- 1 teaspoon of coconut extract
- 1 teaspoon pure vanilla extract

INSTRUCTIONS

1. Whip the cream until foamy.
2. Gradually add the powdered sugar while continuing to beat.
3. Add the coconut extract and pure vanilla extract.
4. Beat until stiff peaks form.

COCONUT CREAM PIE COOKIE CUPS

Sugar cookies and coconut cream go perfectly together. The crunchy cookie with the creamy pudding is delicious.

COOKIE CUPS

This praline layer is fabulous in coconut pie but goes well in many pies. It will harden as it cools in the pie crust.

INGREDIENTS

- 1 cup butter, softened
- 1-1/2 cups sugar
- 2 eggs
- 3 teaspoons pure vanilla extract
- 2-3/4 cups of all-purpose flour
- 1 teaspoon baking powder
- 1 teaspoon salt
- 1/2 cup white chocolate chips

INSTRUCTIONS

1. Preheat the oven to 350 degrees. Spray two regular-size muffin tins with cooking spray.
2. In a stand mixer, cream together the butter and sugar until fluffy.
3. Add eggs and continue beating until incorporated.
4. Mix in the vanilla.
5. Sift together the dry ingredients.
6. Add the flour, baking powder, and salt just until combined.
7. Use a regular ice cream scoop (3 tablespoons) and scoop dough into muffin tins.
8. Bake for 12 minutes. The edges will be slightly golden.
9. Remove from the oven and use a tablespoon, small round lid, or container to press an indention in the middle of the hot cookie.
10. Melt the white chocolate chips in the microwave for 15 seconds and stir until smooth.
11. Brush the melted white chocolate chips on the bottom of the warm cookie cups.
12. Cool for ten minutes in the pan.
13. Remove from the pan and place on a large baking sheet.
14. Cool completely.

TIP

The melted chocolate acts as a barrier to keep the cookie cups from getting soggy. Best if eaten on the same day.

COCONUT CREAM PIE FILLING

INGREDIENTS

- 4 egg yolks
- 1/4 cup cornstarch
- 1/8 teaspoon salt
- 2 cups half-and-half
- 3/4 cup sugar
- 2 teaspoons coconut extract
- 2 tablespoons butter
- ½ cup heavy cream

INSTRUCTIONS

1. Heat half-and-half and sugar in the microwave for 3 to 4 minutes. The milk should be steaming but not boiling. Stir the mixture carefully. It may have air bubbles.
2. In a separate bowl, whisk egg yolks until a pale-yellow color. Whisk in cornstarch and salt with the egg yolks. Once the egg yolks and cornstarch are light and smooth, it's ready for the half-and-half.
3. Place a silicone mat or a towel under your bowl to prevent it from slipping. Slowly drizzle a cup of the warm milk over the egg mixture while constantly whisking. Use one hand to drizzle the milk into the egg yolks and one hand to whisk the mixture. Whisk in the remaining warm milk.
4. Pour the mixture into a clean pot and whisk over medium heat until it thickens.
5. Cook while whisking until the pudding starts bubbling and is thick. Be sure to whisk in the corners of the pot. Use a silicone spatula to clean the sides of the pot periodically. The custard will burn if left on the sides.
6. Remove from the heat at 175 to 180 F. degrees. After coating the back of a spoon and swiping your finger through the custard. It should remain separated.
7. Add butter and coconut extract.
8. Whisk until the butter is melted and incorporated.
9. Press a piece of plastic wrap onto the surface of the pudding to prevent skin from forming. Let it cool at room temperature before placing it in the cookie cups.
10. When ready to serve, whip the heavy cream and fold one cup into the pudding.
11. Pipe or spoon the pudding into the cookie cups.
12. Pipe a dollop of whipped cream on each cookie cup.
13. Sprinkle with toasted coconut.

WHIPPED TOPPING

INGREDIENTS

- 1-1/2 cup heavy whipping cream
- 1/2 cup powdered sugar
- 1 teaspoon coconut extract
- 1 teaspoon pure vanilla extract

INSTRUCTIONS

1. Beat whipped cream at high-speed using an electric mixer until foamy. Gradually add the powdered sugar while continuing to beat.
2. Add the coconut extract and pure vanilla extract.
3. Beat until stiff peaks form.
4. Pipe or spoon pudding into cookie cups.
5. When ready to serve, top cookies and pudding with whipped cream and toasted coconut.

TOASTED COCONUT RECIPE

INGREDIENTS

- 1/3 cup coconut

INSTRUCTIONS

1. Spread coconut on a baking sheet and bake at 350 F. degrees for 10 to 15 minutes. Watch the coconut very closely. Don't let it burn.

TROPICAL DREAM CAKE

Are you dreaming of a tropical vacation? Let this Tropical Dream Cake take you there. Although the cake is made from scratch, the filling is a box of pudding and canned pineapple. The homemade yellow cake is moist and tender and covered with creamy coconut pudding and pineapple. Before serving, add the whipped topping, toasted, and toasted macadamias. It's best to eat after the tropical cream has had a chance to seep into the cake.

MADE-FROM-SCRATCH YELLOW CAKE

INGREDIENTS

- 1/2 cup butter softened
- 1/2 cup vegetable oil
- 1-3/4 cup sugar
- 4 large eggs, room temperature
- 1 tablespoon pure vanilla extract
- 3 cups all-purpose flour, 390 grams
- 1 tablespoon baking powder
- 1/2 teaspoon salt
- 1-1/4 cup buttermilk

INSTRUCTIONS

1. Preheat the oven to 350 degrees.
2. Prepare a 9 x 13 baking pan with baking spray.
3. Whisk the flour, salt, and baking powder.
4. Using a mixer, cream the butter, oil, and sugar until creamy, 3 - 4 minutes.
5. Add the eggs one at a time. Combine well before adding the next egg.
6. Blend in the vanilla.
7. Add half of the dry ingredients into the mixer just until combined.
8. Add the buttermilk and mix just until combined.
9. Blend in the other half of the dry ingredients by hand. The batter may have some small lumps. This will help prevent over-mixing.
10. Pour the batter into the prepared baking pan.
11. Bake for 25 minutes or until a toothpick inserted in the center is mostly clean. The cake should spring back when touched.
12. Cool before poking holes in it.
13. Once the cake has cooled completely, poke holes about 1/2 inch apart all over the cake. Use the back of a wooden spoon.

CAKE TOPPING

INGREDIENTS

- 1 (20 oz.) can of crushed pineapple, drained, keep the juice
- 1-1/4 cup cold milk
- 1 (5.1oz.) package of instant coconut pudding or vanilla
- 8 ounces of frozen whipped topping
- 1/3 cup toasted coconut
- 1/4 cup toasted sliced almonds or macadamia nuts, chopped

INSTRUCTIONS

1. Drain the crushed pineapple and measure out one cup.
2. Spread the pineapple with some of the juice evenly on the cake.
3. Whisk the instant coconut pudding mix with one cup of reserved pineapple juice and cold milk.
4. Evenly distribute the pudding over the pineapple.
5. Spread the whipped topping over the pudding layer.
6. Sprinkle the top of the cake with toasted coconut and toasted almonds.
7. Store covered in the refrigerator.

TROPICAL PINEAPPLE PIE

No-Bake Tropical Pineapple Pie is the perfect summer treat. It's easy to make using cream cheese and canned pineapple. This pie is beautiful when adding pineapple slices around the edge of the pie. Elevate it even more with a small amount of yellow whipped cream and a cherry on top.

GRAHAM CRACKER COCONUT CRUST

INGREDIENTS

- 1-1/4 cups graham cracker crumbs
- 1/4 cup sweetened coconut flakes
- 6 tablespoons melted butter
- 1/4 cup brown sugar

INSTRUCTIONS

1. Preheat the oven to 350 F. degrees.
2. Combine graham cracker crumbs and coconut flakes.
3. Add the melted butter and sugar to your crumbs and combine.
4. Press over the bottom and sides of the 9-inch-deep dish pie.
5. Bake 350 F. degree oven for 10 minutes.
6. Cool completely before adding the filling.

PINEAPPLE FILLING

INGREDIENTS

- 1-1/2 cup heavy cream
- 1/2 cup confectioners' sugar
- 1 teaspoon vanilla
- 1 teaspoon coconut extract
- 8-ounces of cream cheese
- 1/2 cup sugar
- 20-ounce can of crushed pineapple, well-drained, save the juice
- 1 cup sweetened coconut

INSTRUCTIONS

1. Drain the pineapple.
2. Whip the heavy cream, confectioners' sugar, vanilla, and coconut extract until stiff peaks.
3. In a different bowl, mix the cream cheese and sugar until smooth.
4. Fold the whipped cream mixture into the cream cheese mixture.
5. Stir in the well-drained pineapple, sweetened coconut, and whipped cream.
6. Spread the filling evenly in the pie crust.
7. When ready to serve, decorate the pie with pineapple slices around the edges of the pie. The round side of the pineapple faces out.
8. Using a piping bag and a 1M piping tip, pipe whipped cream around the outside edges of the pie. Next to the sliced pineapple ends.
9. In the center of the pie pipe swirl of whipped cream and add a cherry on top.

WHIPPED TOPPING

INGREDIENTS

- 1/2 cup heavy whipping cream
- 1/4 cup powdered sugar
- 1/2 teaspoon coconut extract
- A couple of drops of yellow gel food coloring
- 1(8-ounces) can of sliced pineapple for decorations

INSTRUCTIONS

1. Whip the heavy cream until foamy. Gradually add the powdered sugar while continuing to beat.
2. Add the coconut extract and beat until stiff peaks form.
3. Stir in the food coloring.

Thank you for purchasing this Dessert Champ Creamy Obsessions cookbook from best-selling author, Diane Roark. As an additional thank you, Diane would like to send you free gifts periodically.

If you'd like to receive:

Newsletters

Updates

New Releases

Announcements

Recipes

Sign up at: https://wandering-butterfly-4036.ck.page/1d860b2617/

Follow Diane at:

Facebook: https://www.facebook.com/recipesforourdailybread/

Instagram: https://www.instagram.com/recipesforourbread/

Other Books By Diane Roark
Heartaches to Blessings
Big Dreams Journal
Forgiveness Journal

https://www.amazon.com/dp/B0BBBVR2RX

ABOUT THE AUTHOR

Baking is messy. So is the story of Diane Roark's life. In her memoir, Heartaches to Blessings, Diane tells the intensely riveting story of how she grew up with an alcoholic mother, was robbed at gunpoint, and had a special need's son who underwent eighteen surgeries and died twice in her arms.

Diane's heartaches also include the struggles raising two of her children with attachment issues and a husband with an alcohol addiction. She chronicles the many trials she faced in honest and raw detail.

The story doesn't end in heartache. Her memoir is about finding God's blessings in the midst of difficult circumstances. It's about how one woman ultimately found God's love in the journey of forgiveness, healing, hope, and joy.

Diane loves to talk about God's blessings, especially competing at the World Food Championships. She has been in the top ten each year against some of the world's best chefs, restaurant teams, and home cooks. She has three rare perfect scores and has received a golden ticket to compete each year.

Her message is that, if God can use her, then he can use anybody. Including you! He has a Big Dream for your life. Dream big and include God in every detail. He loves you and has a plan and a dream for each of you.

Our prayer is that this cookbook will bring you much happiness in preparing these dishes and enjoyment for those who get to eat them.